T

Praise for *Ten Letters*

'Ten Letters is one of the most profound, practical and deeply theological books I have read. Chris Russell in my view is a national treasure. He runs one of the least talked about but most exciting and significant Churches in Britain. These letters let you in on his secret. They show how the Church if it is to be missional must be intimate and pastoral. If it is to be authentic to the faith it must be local and spiritual. Above all Chris offers us a glimpse of an intelligent, mission orientated and Spirit led Church. These are letters to his friends but as we listen in we share in a vision of the future. But the really exciting thing is that this Church actually exists and it is in Reading!'

Peter Ward, Professor of Theology and Ministry,
King's College London

'In case I don't return, whenever I fly anywhere I always write a letter to my children on the night before I leave. I tell them the things that I want them to know more than anything else; about my love for them, and about where this love comes from and how it shapes the universe. In this moving and beautifully written book Chris Russell goes several steps further and says in ten lovely letters the things he wants to say to people he has known and ministered to. His love of life, his vivid and rooted faith, his desire to share with others the things he has received come shining through. And although the letters are addressed to others, each one spoke to my heart too. I'm sure they will do the same for anyone who reads this book. There is a file in my drawer with all my letters to my children in it. I think I will add these ten letters as well.'

Stephen Cottrell, Bishop of Chelmsford

'These letters are honest, thoughtful, caring, engaging, informative, inspiring and life changing.'

J. John, Evangelist

'This book is pure poetry; the kind that shakes you to your core and moves you to a deep place of thinking and being. Uncomfortably real, fiercely honest, beautifully Chris.'

Rachel Gardner, Director, Romance Academy

Ten Letters

to be delivered in the event of my
death

Chris Russell

DARTON · LONGMAN + TODD

First published in 2012 by
Darton, Longman and Todd Ltd
1 Spencer Court
140–142 Wandsworth High Street
London SW18 4JJ

ISBN: 978-0-232-52921-0

A catalogue record for this book is available from the British Library

Typeset by Kerrypress Ltd, Luton, Bedfordshire
Printed and bound in Great Britain by Bell & Bain, Glasgow

To my beloved Belinda,
Hope, Jessie and Dora:
my life is your letter.

Contents

Introduction

My friends will testify, probably without much prompting, that I am prone to being over-dramatic. While this can be seen in a variety of ways, it is particularly evident on the anniversary of my birth. Every birthday I wonder if the year to come will be my last, and I'm filled with a certain element of surprise that I am actually still alive.

For some reason I thought everyone else entertained such wonderings on their birthdays. But my close friends told me the other day that they don't. So I need to make my slight propensity for over-dramatisation work for me – hence this book.

In the letters that follow are the things I really want to say in the event of my death. Some are things I haven't dared to say, felt confident enough to say, or just not got around to. Others have been regular themes in many a conversation. But this is not some manifesto for life; it's addressing particular things to particular people. These are letters which I have written, printed off and signed, and which reside in the top drawer of my desk; the ten letters to be delivered in the event of my death.

They are to particular individuals – some of them are close friends, some are people I vaguely know, a couple are to people I have never even met. To those whose names they bear, I crave your indulgence. Some names have been changed. While they are written as if they are my last words, they are by no means intended to be the last words on these subjects. I'd be interested to hear your replies.

I am grateful to more people than I can mention. Thanks to those who have helped me get this far; to Craig for the kick-off conversation in the garden three years ago and subsequent insider wisdom; to Cathy and those who read random chapters and gave thoughts, to Juliette for reading it all through and making it so much better; to Tom for being the design guru; to David Moloney and Kathy Dyke for taking it on.

Thanks also to dear friends whose conversations continually inspire; Troy and Lis, Brad, Jettie and all our friends at Mars Hill, Christian and Michelle, and to those who have taught me and teach me. And to my parents for their legacy and example, Brian Shenton for his trust, Jim McNeish for his framing and reframing, J John and Killy for being friends of the longest standing, Pete Ward for his conversations, the West Reading Collective for their companionship, and essentially, particularly and beyond all else, the whole community of St Laurence Reading. Gratitude and love to you beyond telling.

This book is dedicated to the best things about me – Belinda, Hope, Jessie and Dora – in inexpressible gratitude.

1

Everything

To Marie

Marie is a yoga-teaching, allotment-owning mother of three hip children. She is married to Nigel, who teaches art and is most surely One of the Nicest People You Could Ever Meet. Of course they drive a VW camper. Together with a couple of other households we form the West Reading Collective.

Marie's roots are in Catholic Malta. She was educated at a Catholic school where the True Faith was literally beaten into her. She tells of being forced to comply with faith as if it were a dictatorial regime, and of finding the whole dogma of organised faith a straitjacket that didn't simply restrict her movements, but imprisoned her. She couldn't wait to be free of it.

As a result she is at best ambivalent towards Christianity. She could easily reject the whole faith based on her experience. But she counts herself as deeply spiritual. Something in her longs for a different framework to understand things by, a new language to be introduced to so she might speak and listen to and of the things of God. The shame is that everything she has, understandably, come to assume about Christianity is wrong.

Dear Marie,

After all those conversations who would have thought, a letter? There is so much I could write about – the allotment, the children and Reading secondary education and possible camp-sites in the south where you can light your own fires. But, it won't surprise you that it's the Christian faith that concerns me most.

I can understand why you've put clear water between you and the faith you were brought up in. If I had been forced to go to confession every week in ill-fitting shoes, or told that if I ate a communion wafer without being worthy it would turn into a snake in my mouth, or been aware of the hypocrisy and abuses of power that were going on, I would want to shake the ecclesiastical dust from my feet too. But what if, rather than that being what Christianity was all about, this was actually a terrible corruption of it? The abuse of the best is the worst. What if everything you have rejected Christianity on and for, is wrong? Or at least twisted? What if the truth of faith looks completely different?

What I want to do is spread out a huge backdrop canvas and sketch out the scope of the Christian faith. I have tried to do this with language we would use in conversations, but forgive me if I tip over into clichés. Obviously I do this from the point of being both convinced and committed to this take on life. But it's bigger than me and my comprehension of it. Here's the plan for this letter: starting at the beginning I will claw back the word 'God', redefining God in the light of God's self- revelation. I will quickly sketch out the implications of this for creation as a whole and us, as those made in God's image. I will suggest that God's dealing with his creatures is that of one bound up with the reality of this life, our relationships, our time and our needs. And that this involvement and commitment is seen supremely in the life, death and resurrection of Jesus. These events of his are world-defining for us. How that definition takes shape in our lives will be explored as I try to coax out a take on the Spirit which does justice to the God of life and the hope that we are invited into for all of our futures. I know it is a bit much – a bit like trying to capture the Niagara Falls in a tea cup.

But if I know anything in life, I know this.

Firstly, God. In our conversations God is the one we usually avoid talking about. But it can't be ducked. What if God is the most misunderstood, misrepresented and miscomprehended word in any language? If you were describing the God you don't believe in what words would you use?

It is often clear to me that when people tell me they don't believe in God, there is a huge variance in what or who we are talking of. When I lived in south London as a curate (think deputy head vicar), the local atheist came to the door of the house which was in turn next door to the church building, and I opened it.

Him: 'Is your dad in?'

Me: 'Hold on, I will just call him. He lives in Coventry.'

Him: 'Oh right, so who are you?'

Me: 'I'm the curate. Think deputy head vicar. Nice to meet you.'

Him: 'Nice to meet you. I'm the Local Atheist.' (He really did call himself that.) 'Anyway, I came to tell you I don't believe in God.'

Me: 'Well, that is certainly good to know. Which God don't you believe in?

Him (slightly flustered as it's not going quite the way he thought): 'I don't believe that God is some old guy, sitting up in the clouds. I don't believe he made the world in six days. I don't believe he punishes people when they do wrong and that he is just up there trying to catch people out. That he sends people to hell and he never does anything to help anyone, or do anything to stop suffering …'

Me: 'Great. I don't believe in that God either.'

It seems all our decks need to be cleared. I was taught by a gentleman of a professor called Nicholas Lash. In his book, *Believing Three Ways in One God*, he wrote:

> It is a lifelong enterprise of learning that there is
> nothing that may easily be said of God; that if we find it
> easy to say certain things of God, the chances are that,
> when we say them, we lose sight of God.

God is not a type. God is not one amongst others. God is not a species. If you had 100 items and added God into the mix you would not then have 101 items. The other day you showed me a book a friend of yours, who is a Quaker, gave to you. In Quakerism there has been a long-standing debate (or is it silence?) about the reality of God. The book, by David Boulton, is entitled: *Real like the daisies, or real like I love you?*, which comes from a question said to have been asked by a child of her Quaker parents: 'Is God real, as things like daisies and elephants and mountains are real, or real like love, justice, beauty and truth?' The short answer is surely 'Yes'. The complicated answer is 'real like God'.

But what does that mean? The trouble is, there are as many different understandings of what God might mean as there are people. And the history of philosophy is full of those who have sought to define God ('the one greater than which nothing can be conceived' as Aquinas says), in concepts: long words like omniscience, omnipotence, omnipresence and omnibenevolence, which, to be honest, leave most of us none the wiser.

So Marie, imagine we are sitting in Workhouse Coffee following the school drop-off on Friday morning. I order my usual double espresso. You're having some nonsense decaff-peppermint-and-steamed-soya latte. The real drink sits steaming in the middle of the, fairly wobbly, table. In attempting to talk accurately about God, the twentieth-century philosopher Ludwig Wittgenstein poured out a cup of freshly ground coffee before his students. He asked one of them to describe the smell of coffee. When his volunteer was unable to do so, Wittgenstein said something like this: 'If we haven't got the correct words to accurately describe the smell of coffee which we can hold in a cup in our hands, how can we think we have the words to accurately describe God?'

And I would be with him entirely if it wasn't for Jesus.

For in this one, God stands before us and gives us the words so we might describe him truly. For Christianity clears the table of the long words, the preconceived ideas, the philosophical concepts, and sets before us a young Jewish Palestinian man. My all-time favourite theologian, Karl Barth makes the running when he says in his *Epistle to the Romans* that Jesus explodes our definitions of God. And all that we can say that might be true is said from the side of the crater which has been caused by the explosion of this shell of his self revelation.

God is not some philosophical idea to be grasped or grappled with. But one who addresses us. It is not we who make the moves to find and discover God; it is God who moves to find and discover us. We work out what can be said about God in the light of what God has enabled us to say, what he has revealed to us.

Only God can reveal God.

Because of Jesus we talk of God's being in relationship. A few pages in and we're at the Trinity.

God is not an individual with a nature, a cosmic being with a substance, but Father, Son and Spirit existing and being in loving relationship. This is the God who is revealed in Jesus. One who can only be talked of truly when three are referred to. One who is the ultimate parent who creates and cherishes in love, one who is Son, brought into being by the Father and constantly giving himself in selfless love, and Spirit who goes between and upholds Father and Son, enabling, empowering and bring life. God is three, God is one. God's oneness, God's unity comes from these three distinctions, persons if you like, co-existing and existing totally for and because of each other. There is no substance behind this God, and no greater reality. There is nothing this God is forced to do to be God, nothing that is lacking in this God's life, nothing that is beyond this God. God is love because Father loves Son loves Spirit loves Father loves Spirit loves Son. And so with all this talk of love the resonances start for us; as Eugene Peterson says in his book *Christ Plays in Ten Thousand Places*: 'If God is revealed as personal, the only way that God can be known is in a personal response.'

This is who God is in God's very self. Obviously we are just at the beginning of things, teetering on the edge of the mystery, it is not who we know God to be so much that counts, but who God knows Godself to be. But because of Jesus what we have glimpsed is true.

This God brings life into being. It is not so much an event as an action which sets up a relationship. Through no external need

(God wouldn't have been any less God if God had chosen not to create), through no pressure or force (this is a free act) God chooses to bring into being something other than Godself. He does this from nothing. When your husband Nigel paints something or makes a sculpture, he uses materials. We can only make things from things. God, however, brings into being everything from nothing. A few things to think about:

- From what they know of our Milky Way galaxy, scientists have guestimated that a galaxy contains from one billion to one trillion stars. They also believe that there are about ten billion galaxies in the universe. So, there may be as many as 10,000,000,000,000,000,000,000,000 stars in the universe.
- No two zebras are the same in their markings.
- 50,000 of the cells in your body will die and be replaced by new cells, all while you have been reading this sentence.
- Did you see that penguin film?
- Concentrate on your breath. What does life feel like? What kind of gift is this?
- How does singing happen?

God has brought into being this unfathomably immense universe of which we are but a speck. God is the composer of sunlight and tides, sperm whales and Saturn, dragonflies and nerve endings. God created this world with joy and tenderness, with astonishing beauty and complexity, with passion and silence, with stunning awe and delicacy. This world is not God, but it is God's. There is not a square inch, not a living being or plant, not an asteroid or distant sun, that God doesn't lay claim to. The God who speaks all things into being in the Genesis poem is responsible for everything. And then there is the stuff we can't see that impacts us – tides and gravity, inertia and genetic sequences, seasons and magnetic fields.

And it's good and blessed. 'The earth is the Lord's and everything in it' (Psalm 24:1). All truth is his truth, all beauty is his beauty, all goodness is his goodness. And everything is given freely, as a gift. 'What have we got that we have not received?' (1 Corinthians 4:7). As Rowan Williams writes in *Tokens of Trust*:

> Within every circumstance, every object, every person, God's action is going on ... A sort of white heat at the heart of everything ...

Humanity is formed and breathed into with God's own breath. We are made with the capacity for producing Mozart and Rothko, Durham Cathedral and democracy, bicycles and rope, key-hole surgery and *Avatar*, champagne and Quavers (surely the tastiest of crisps). We are fearfully and wonderfully made, with the capacity not only to create and produce, but to love and be loved. Because the maker makes us in his image.

A fractal is a pattern that is seen recurring throughout a structure, from the largest to the smallest part. Think of snow-flakes – they have a pattern as a whole when you put them under your microscope (this is taken on trust as mine always melt under that little light). But look closer and you see the same pattern reproduced on each arm of the flake, then zoom in closer and you see the same pattern in minutiae. Think of a pine tree – the tree takes a shape, the branch takes the same shape, the leaf takes the same shape and the pattern of the leaf takes the same shape. These patterns go through creation. They also go through us.

A moment ago, I said that the very least that we know about God is God is three in one, Father, Son and Spirit existing in mutual life, loving, giving, preferring, honouring, and praising. God is love because the three are in loving relationship. Men and women are made to replicate this God in loving relationships. Being made in God's image means that we are fractals for the divine life which lies at the heart of all things, all mysteries, all that is. For at the heart of all things is not some impersonal force, but three persons in loving relationship. This fractal of relation-ship is his hallmark on us. Community, love, care, sacrifice, kindness, tenderness, commitment, faithfulness, joy, companion-ship is what we're about, because it's what God is about. So when

Hayley, a seventeen-year-old who is out of school and employment convinces us to take her with us to Uganda to do something for those who have nothing and gets turned inside out by it, this is the image of God in her. When Kirsty spends all her wages making sure her blood relatives are cared for, since neither of her parents work and her mother is physically disabled, this is the image of God in her. When Alison up the road weeps at any death, when Paul works three days for free to make sure strangers' costs are covered, when Vic and Nathan perpetually put themselves out to foster children, when Saskia won't give up hoping, this is the image of God in them. And there is nothing more beautiful.

—m—

These then are the first decisive sketches on the backdrop. These are the origins of who we are, our Genesis. Once again the wonderful Nicholas Lash comments in *Believing* that the Christian story:

> ... does not simply say where the world comes from and where it is being brought, but where I come from and hope to go to. If it is a story, then, it is not only the story of the world, but it is also autobiographical in character. It is profoundly personal testimony.

The autobiography makes hard reading. Not that we are under any illusions (we know things aren't as they should be), but the story tells of the misuse of the freedom that God gave. The creation poem tells how the first humans were enticed by the idea that they could be gods themselves; they could be the judges, they could live in God's world with themselves as autonomous, self-regulating beings. Life without God, as our own gods. We have been making the same choice every day since. We love setting ourselves up as judges over others, we declare ourselves innocent and other guilty; we have a default setting in choosing for ourselves. God might have made us with the capacity for wonderful production of music, beauty and wisdom, but we also have the capacity for Hiroshima, Auschwitz, chemical warfare, CO_2 emissions and abuse of children.

All of us swim in these waters (or are they sewers?) of self-obsession. We might be made as fractals of the divine relationship but our hearts have got curved in on themselves, and that affects all of us, in all ways. Instead of loving others before ourselves, we love ourselves before others. We live in a society that has replaced soul with self. This is not how it was meant to be. Deep in our hearts we feel the fracture of that. When you go against the grain you get splinters.

God, however, doesn't leave us to it; he doesn't shrug and move on. No, faithfulness and freedom to love and commit whatever the cost are seen in God's ways with the world. For we don't get to know God in the abstract, but in the concrete, in God's history, God's story, within the world. When Yuri Gagarin, the Soviet astronaut, returned in triumph from being the first man in orbit in 1967, he declared that any religion was deluded, as he had been up to the heavens and not seen God there. But 'If you haven't seen God on earth you will never see him in heaven,' as Metropolitan Anthony wrote in *School of Prayer*.

In the garden of the world, God went searching for his rebellious creatures. The charm offensive was to be led by a small insignificant family. This family were chosen to be the bearers of the map for the route back into relationship with God. A risky choice, but this God works through the particular for the universal. They are chosen to tell everyone they are chosen; they are blessed to bring all people blessing. They are God's people, not that others aren't, but their particular vocation is to be his light in an increasingly dark world, to be the signpost pointing to God, to be a channel of his peace. When they are enslaved, God frees them, when they are starving, he feeds them, when they are lost he guides them, when they are landless he opens the way to their promised land. They are given laws to help them to live, songs to sing, prophets to correct them, and more get-out-of-jail-free cards than they can hold.

But time and time again they do what we all do. We all use the vocation and gifts of God for our own sake rather than for what they were given for – others. None of this lessens God's side of the relationship; God continues loving, forgiving, recreating, championing, and protecting. But it's clear it isn't going to work – these people are not the answer.

They have become part of the problem.

—〰—

God makes things new by doing something from nothing. Again. A teenage virgin becomes pregnant, God's word turns to flesh. God's word has to learn to speak the language of humanity, the hands that formed stars grasp his mother's hair, the one who provided food for all living things is nursed at the breast. Here God shows us truly what God is like and truly what humans should be like. Messiah. Not produced by our own efforts or evolution. But through God's intervention.

Of course everyone tries to co-opt him. Everyone wants their own messiah. Especially one who will back them. So we know of rich man's Jesus and revolutionaries' Jesus, of Family Values Jesus and Bohemian Jesus, of western Jesus and cosmic Jesus, of ecclesiastical Jesus and just-a-good-man Jesus. As Wittgenstein said, 'I had a picture of Jesus and it held me captive.' Untrue pictures of Jesus do that. But his true face does something opposite. For if you truly look at him, you don't so much see your own reflection, but someone who is alike but utterly other, the same but profoundly different. And this one lived as no one else lived. Dostoevsky, quoted in Brother Emile's book, *Never a Stranger*, talks about Jesus as if he has fallen in love:

> There is only one face which is absolutely beautiful –
> the face of Christ – and the appearance of his infinitely,
> incommensurably beautiful face is an endless miracle.

Jesus lived life in its fullness. Not because he had everything the shekel could buy, not because he enjoyed extensive world travel, or played fast and loose. He lived fully because he lived freely. Freely because he didn't care what people thought of him. He was free to love those no one else would dream of going near: sex-workers, swindlers, those with contagious diseases. When he washed feet, touched lepers and stopped the world for beggars, this was not a PR opportunity; he was demonstrating what God is truly like. He drew near to people to lead them into the kingdom of God. This kingdom is one in which 5,000 people were miraculously fed, because in God's kingdom no one is hungry; it's one in which those whose legs are beyond use with debilitating conditions are made strong and can dance; it's one where waves are stilled, fears are calmed, and the dead are raised. This kingdom is the place the world should be. It's where God reigns. And being religious gets you no nearer to it.

But Jesus doesn't just come to tell us all is well, it's all just fine, it's all peace. The world is not at peace. I remember once when you knocked me flying as you rode your bike up the pavement on the way to a yoga lesson you were teaching. It was clear you had had a terrible morning. I think there might have been some shouting. And your only words to me were: 'Out of the way, Chris, it's been a bad morning. Shanti bloody shanti.' What we need is not just exercises and techniques. What we need is for our situation to change. And religious or non-religious practice won't do it.

In fact, being religious caused many to hate Jesus. We know there are few times people will fight harder and dirtier than when their investment, their control, their access, their influence and power in the divine is slipping from their hands. Jesus gave himself over to this. He walked into the trap knowing exactly what was going to happen. One of the most fascinating things about the gospel accounts of Jesus is that, on the one hand, people were doing horrendous things to Jesus – lying about him, capturing him, putting him through a kangaroo court with jumped-up charges, mocking him, torturing him, inflicting unbearable pain on him, killing him. Yet on the other hand we see Jesus in control all the way through. As if this is what he chose to happen. Not for his sake, but for others. It's a human thing to save your life; it's a godly thing to lay down your life for others.

So the cross of Jesus is hoisted at the centre of human life and divine love. I do wonder whether we are quite aware of the potency and implications of wearing a diamond-encrusted execution tool around our necks. But I guess the power in this cross derives entirely from the events of his death. What it means is what happened. Jesus died because Judas betrayed him for money, because Judas kissed him without meaning it, because Peter, despite his best intentions, betrayed his promise, because the religious leaders were threatened and lied, because the disciples ran off, because the crowd, swayed by peer pressure, changed their fickle minds, because Pilate was too cowardly to do something people wouldn't like, because the soldiers just did their job, and because everyone who was crucified did die.

Jesus died because we betray each other, because we kiss without meaning it, because we break promises, because we lie, because we don't do what we should, because we are fickle and swayed by others, because we are unjust, because we are cruel, because we are scared, because what we did to him we do to each other. And worse still, when we get our hands on him, we do it to God. But he died for even stronger reasons than these: he went that way because he chose to go that way.

> Were you there when the crucified my Lord?
> Were you there when they crucified my Lord?
> Oh, sometimes it causes me to tremble, tremble,
>   tremble.
> Were you there when they crucified my Lord?

Along with those slaves in the cotton-picking fields in the deep south we sing, with tears streaming down our face, that we were there, because this death was not just his death, it was our death, it was my death. As Rowan Williams writes in *Tokens of Trust:*

> This is what your untruth means; you have been offered unconditional mercy and you turn from it in loathing.

You have come to the place where you cannot recognise
life for what it is. You don't know the difference
between life and death. The reality is that you are dead.

The one who breathed into the first humans that they might have
his life and live, breathes his last. So we might have his life and
live. Here is love; before we even turned to him, we are loved to
death; accepted, forgiven, embraced, and remade. The great
exchange takes place; he takes my place at the greatest personal
cost, so I might take his place freely. His death for my life.

Suffering, pain, alienation, god-forsakenness are now taken
up into God's life and realm of experience. No one suffers alone –
there is a man of sorrows, one familiar with suffering, who shares
the worst of what we as humans go through. He is laid in a
borrowed tomb and heaven and earth wait in silence with an
inaudible sigh of despair.

Yet three days later something happens. David Ford in *The
Shape of Living* describes this as an event greater than which
nothing can be imagined. In that tomb something happens to
that particular body.

Actually not just something, just one thing; resurrection.

It has never happened to anyone else before or since. It is a
God-sized event; the work of the Father in the power of the
Spirit on the Son. It's an *ex nihilo* event. From nothing. And it
takes place at the dawn in a garden. Resurrection is not revival, or
a coming back to life – some kind of divine charge-the-paddles
resuscitation – it is the in-breaking of new life; the life of the
promised Kingdom, the life of the future in the here and now.
David Ford again:

> There is no ready-made worldview into which it fits. As
> a God-sized event, the same considerations apply to it as
> to the reality of God: if we think we have a framework
> that contains is, then we have not grasped the sort of
> event it is.

For the next forty days this Jesus touched this present world with future resurrection life. Uncommonly for me, I think about it in terms of the tangents in Year 9 maths:

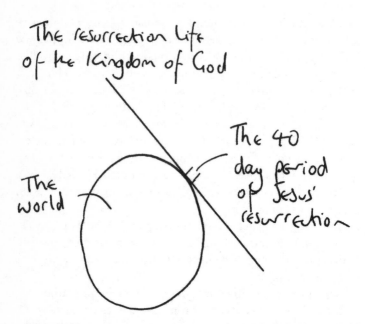

The forty days of Jesus' resurrection is this grazing of the present against the future. He is the firstborn from the dead; he is the guarantee of what will one day be for all God's people; he is the model for what will one day be. So he is the same, yet transformed; he is recognisable but changed: he can eat and talk, cook and engage, touch and be touched. He is hyper-real, resurrection-real; he passes through walls because his reality is stronger and truer than the wall. Those in C. S. Lewis' *The Great Divorce* who journey to heaven cut their bare feet on the grass because the grass is so real, and have to wear dark glasses because the colours are too vibrant.

Because of the resurrection of this one who had been dead, killed in a godforsaken, cruel torture, the cross is transformed from tragedy to victory, from ugly to beautiful, from the place where everything is lost to the place where everything is given. As Rowan Williams writes in *Tokens of Trust*, the ricochet created by Jesus' life is profound:

> This man's life suggests, no stronger than that, insists that nowhere is God absent, powerless or irrelevant. There is no situation in the universe in the face of which God is at a loss.

The death and resurrection of Jesus stand as the focal point, the pivot of all history. The significance and implications of it are impossible to overemphasise; indeed the fractals of dying and rising, of sacrifice and gift, of self-denial and gaining your soul, of love enduring through death, of light being stronger than darkness, goodness stronger than hatred, of death, sadness, grief, evil, violence, torture, separation, cruelty, injustice not having the last word.

So, as David Ford writes, 'joy may be a greater scandal than evil, suffering or death.'

—w—

But this event in and of itself doesn't impact me and you, truly, it doesn't 'take' in us, until we join in with it. Until we die with him, so we can rise with him. Until we take our last breath for ourselves, and receive the living breath of this one who was dead and is now alive again. So once Jesus has returned to be in God's space, heaven, after the forty days of resurrection, the Spirit comes to make God's people live. This group of people breathe the same air that Jesus breathed; Christ becomes the atmosphere in which we live – God's intense, enfleshed presence, not bound to a single body, but taking flesh in young men and old women, in children and teenagers. The Spirit is God present to us, for us, in us, apart from us bringing the conditions of the future resurrection kingdom into the present world. Any attempt to manage the life and work of the Spirit in relation to our lives must be ruled out. There is something fundamentally disturbing,

overwhelming, stretching, disconcerting, disarming and invigor-
ating about the tenderest of the Spirit's interactions with us. For
here the messiah from Nazareth comes alive to me and for me.

The Spirit makes the church be, bringing a community into
being that bears the name of the Saviour and seeks to fulfil the
particular vocation to be his light in an increasingly dark world,
to be the signpost pointing to a living God, to be a channel of his
peace. The Spirit is no way a possession of this church; still less are
his works synonymous with what the church does. It would be a
recasting of everything we know about Jesus to suggest he was
represented on this earth by some highly formalised, structural,
authoritarian, hierarchical group of men (which, let's face it, the
majority of the church is). Yet in service and love, in prayer and
wonder, in breaking bread and sharing wine as the sign of
participating in his death, and being overwhelmed in the waters
of baptism as a sign of rising with him, this people bear his name,
are a fractal of his life, pre-evidence of his community, servants of
the kingdom that is always worth investing in because it will last
for ever. Of course the kingdom of God is far bigger than the
boundaries of the church – but all goodness, all justice, all acts of
kindness and generosity, all healing and hope, all beauty and
creativity are echoes of this kingdom which the rumour of the
resurrection and vigour of the Spirit pledge as true.

—m—

The canvas has little room left for more shapes or colour, yet here
it starts revealing a whole new vision. Beyond this there is more
than can be conceived. In the last book of scripture, the profound
and dangerous Revelation of John, the one who was dead but is
now alive again draws the history of this present age to a close
with these words: 'Behold I make all things new' (Revelation
21:5). Not just some things, not just a few things, but all things.
Scripture begins with all things being made, and ends opening up
a whole new realm of re-creation. This is redemption, a rework-
ing of what is already in existence as the raw material for the
eternal. Redemption takes place not in some other place, but in

this place. In this world of torture and crosses, killing fields and gas chambers, industrial scorched waste-land and plundered rain forests, concrete jungles and unmarked graves. It is this world, this earth that is charged with eternal potential. God is not into escape or destruction, but into reconciling all things, renewing all things and restoring all things.

The promise is that the full realisation of God's Kingdom will begin with the maker pronouncing and enacting judgement. As Miroslac Volf writes in *Exclusion and Embrace*:

> God will judge, not because God gives people what they deserve, but because some people refuse to receive what no one deserves; if evildoers experience God's terror, it will not be because they have done evil, but because they have resisted to the end the powerful lure of the open arms of the crucified messiah.

Judgment is good, good news. But meeting God face to face is always a moment of judgment for us. And scripture doesn't try to tone down the advice that we should be ready and trembling.

So maybe you can begin to see that Christianity isn't a message – it is contact. It's like running into a room shouting 'Fire!' Or whispering in a beloved's ear, 'Will you marry me?' We are being asked for a response, to come and take our place in the great drama of life with his canvas as our backdrop. It is costly and life-changing, it is all encompassing and demanding, it's fulfilling and delightful. For once you have tasted, you cannot live without this God.

Marie, you thirst for living, not just existing; you're dissatisfied with fakes and imitations; you want to plumb the depths and reach the heights. Maybe that's why you rejected the faith you were nurtured in. But the true God invites you to live true life. Offering you a thousand new starts in the comprehension of God, yourself, the goodness and depravity of this world, the defining life, death and resurrection of Jesus, the life-giving Spirit and transforming community of the church, and the hope of a life beyond this that no eye has seen no ear has heard and no heart could be adequately be prepared for.

The everything you desire is found in God.

I would have loved to have known your thoughts.

Chris

2

Faith

To Eddie

Although I only know him vaguely, Eddie seems nice and steady. He is part of the leadership team of a small but lively church. To be honest, he is someone I don't feel that at ease with, partly because I feel a bit extrovert and dramatic around him, but mainly because I feel on a bit of a different spiritual wavelength to him; he's in glorious DAB radio, and I'm on crackly old medium wave. His ministry seems to exist with very set ideas, clear flow charts, and easy explanations or obvious solutions.

I wouldn't count him as a friend, but my heart goes out to him, and I have never told him why. Two years ago I happened to be at a prayer meeting with other church leaders when Eddie told us that his father had been moved into a hospice for the last stages of his life. That very week the mother of my closest friend had died of cancer, so it was all very close to home for me. Eddie shared his conviction, through tears, that in recent days he had been challenged to have more faith, and now in the light of this challenge, was certain that if he truly believed, his father, presently in the palliative cares stages of cancer, would be miraculously healed and live. He told the hushed gathering that God was disappointed with how little faith we all had, but to exercise faith he was, directly, going to leave the prayer meeting, go to his father's hospice and declare that he would be healed.

It seemed that everyone liked what he said. Except me.

Dear Eddie,

I am so sorry that your father died. I can't imagine how difficult those last weeks were when you believed, prayed and hoped for a different outcome. Ever since I was part of the prayer meeting where you shared your challenge to have more faith, your situation and the leading you felt within it has been churning over again and again in my mind. My sense is that at heart this brings into focus the question of what faith actually is.

Maybe I should have said this face to face, but writing it helps me set it all out before you, so you might be able to see the whole picture of my argument. Basically I want to say the following things: firstly, that the question of what 'faith' actually *is* is pivotal to everything we hold to as Christians, and secondly, that faith is a gift we receive rather than it being something we *do*. Then I'll explore the difference receiving this gift makes, and argue that it looks like radical trust.

It seems to me that true faith is opposed most strongly by fear, and by a counterfeit idea that faith works like magic. This in reality militates against true faith. Rather, the ingredients of true faith-full living are life with others, sacrifice and facing death with hope. I want to keep in front of me the life-and-death situations that your family and mine, those we love and those we come into contact with, face year in, year out. What is said needs to be said into the context of our mortal lives.

I don't want to over-talk the game. But on this one the stakes couldn't be higher. Whether it's in vast basilicas, dusty leprosy mission outposts, secret persecuted underground meetings or as the flames licked up the martyrs' pyres, Christianity hinges on what faith is. It's a foundational understanding that we don't get anywhere with God through what we do, through how devout or religious we are, through how good or well-meaning we are, through how many songs we can lip-synch to, or through our ability to recite the books of the Bible in a natty rhyme. No, God's grace is given to us not by anything we do but through faith. Good news.

However, my guess would be that if you or I were asked if we felt we had enough faith, we would both answer unhesitatingly: 'No'. To talk of faith is to raise a subject that makes most of us feel bad, inferior, and found wanting. It's something we feel a lack of. Because we walk around sensing that if we had more, things would be different; with God, with each other, with this world, and with ourselves. We crane our necks, looking upwards at those giants of faith who do things like get on boats without knowing where they will get off, fly around the world telling us stories of wonders and signs, and foresee the future as a time when streets are full of people worshipping.

The way that many of us talk, you could be forgiven for assuming that having faith is something you need to do, acquire, summon up, conjure up, will yourself to get more of, because you most certainly haven't got enough of it. In the leaps of faith, those who can will themselves to jump the furthest get the loudest applause and the biggest prize.

So it's worth quoting from Lewis Carroll's *Alice Through the Looking Glass* (although I don't know about you, but I have never really got on with the books, let alone the films):

> Alice laughed. 'There's no use trying,' she said; 'one *can't* believe impossible things.'
>
> 'I daresay you haven't had much practice,' said the Queen. 'When I was younger, I always did it for half an hour a day. Why, sometimes I've believed as many as six impossible things before breakfast.'

For too many people, both within and outside the camp, Christian faith is about believing impossible, unbelievable things. Rowan Williams addresses this in *Tokens of Trust* when he says that many people assume that when we talk of having faith in God, it's '… as if God were the name of one more doubtful thing like UFOs or ghosts to add to the list of the furniture of my imagination'. Hence there are myriads of people who left any faith in God behind when they gave up believing in Father Christmas. Maybe this isn't helped by the fact that in many people's minds they look rather alike.

My opener to you would be that faith is not about opinions, about willing ourselves to believe, or about rational assent to statements of fact. Bluntly, it cannot be about my ability to make myself believe difficult things, as I somehow force myself to suspend critical faculties and believe something unbelievable. Because, if it is, then Christianity is a religion of works – it is something we make happen, we do, we cause by assent to dogmatic statements or hopeful wishes. And I can't be doing with that because every sinew of Jesus' body held out that this wonderful thing we call salvation is a gift.

Faith isn't something we do, but a gift we receive.

Now we exercise faith each and every day in many and diverse situations. If I get on the number 17 bus over to the other side of Reading, I show faith that it will take me the way that the number 17's route goes. If I get on a train to the London, I exercise faith that this train will take me to the specified destination, although I have rather less faith this will happen at the advertised time. Now, my having faith that these modes of transport will get me to where I need to get to doesn't make them go that way. I don't create the thing by this faith. But I get in on it by faith.

I wonder if I could set out a different take on a familiar story from the gospels, staying with the transport theme, but this time using a boat. It's the infamous story of Peter walking on the water. You'll remember that Jesus had dismissed the crowds and sent the disciples over to the other side of the lake. But a ferocious storm blew up and the boat was in danger of sinking. To save you having to grab a Bible, here are the key verses:

> Shortly before dawn Jesus went out to them, walking on the lake. When the disciples saw him walking on the lake, they were terrified. 'It's a ghost,' they said, and cried out in fear.

> But Jesus immediately said to them: 'Take courage! It is I. Don't be afraid.'

> 'Lord, if it's you,' Peter replied, 'tell me to come to you on the water.'

'Come,' he said.

> Then Peter got down out of the boat, walked on the
> water and came toward Jesus. But when he saw the
> wind, he was afraid and, beginning to sink, cried out,
> 'Lord, save me!'

> Immediately Jesus reached out his hand and caught him.
> 'You of little faith,' he said, 'why did you doubt?'
> (*Matthew 14:25–31*)

This passage is the one you spoke from that day at the prayer
meeting, drawing out the challenge of Peter's faith. I've done the
same. The gist of what we say is always something like: 'Check
out the faith that Peter showed. We should be like him. Let's get
out of the boat. Without buoyancy aids.' Books have been
written on this. I have heard one preacher having a go at the
other disciples for staying in the boat. Having a go at them as if
they were in the room. In this scheme of things faith is taking
risks, that venturing into the realm of the unbelievable. This was
the story you used to suggest you should get out of the boat of
unbelief that your dad was going to die, and in faith claim that he
would instead live. Getting out of the boat was telling him it
wasn't going to be. It was a real risk. But faith is shown in walking
in water.

I'm sorry Eddie, but I think this gets the passage all wrong. To
cut to the chase, I think if Peter had really exercised faith he
would have stayed in the boat. (Just in case you think I'm going
completely off the rails with my reading of this passage, I'd like to
add that John Calvin and Karl Barth also have this take on it,
although that might make you even less convinced.)

In terms of the text everything hinges around the rebuke by
Jesus, 'You of little faith, why did you doubt?' Now in the
retelling many will suggest that once out of the boat what Peter
doubted was that he could walk on the water; it was the waves
and the wind that made him doubt. But that's not there in the
text. From the narrative, the only thing he clearly doubts is that it

was Jesus in the first place. Jesus has come to them in the middle of a storm. They are clearly and justifiably terrified. He greets them with: 'Take courage, it is I. Don't be afraid.' Here comes Peter's doubt: 'Lord if it's you, tell me to come to you on the water.' The only thing we are told he doubts is that it really was Jesus. And his lack of faith is shown by his need for proof, which is why he asks to walk on the water.

In the middle of the storm and the waves and the swell, pounded by uncertainty and fear and concern, to have exercised faith would have been to trust Jesus words that he need not fear, and so despite the extreme conditions, not to have asked to get out of the boat. Faith would have been trusting that Jesus was actually with them.

You see, rather than faith being something we do, we conjure up, we make happen, I wonder if faith is actually about trust. And trust not in what he can do for us, but in who he is, and in the true words he speaks to us.

But, as you and I know, trust is a tricky old thing. These days trust is not the universal currency it once was. We are notoriously suspicious: of our historic institutions, of our representatives, of systems and establishments that should serve us, and of each other. Breaches of trust are exposed each day by a media that we do not trust. Families and relationships are broken by actions that destroy trust. So it is little surprise that on the world stage diplomats, peacemakers and leaders engage in a complicated and protracted dance of mistrust.

It is in such a world of storms that Jesus holds out the gift of faith to us: 'Take courage, it is I. Do not be afraid.' And in so doing Jesus creates faith; faith being the belief that God is present, that his intentions towards me are loving and good, that he is the most profound player in the drama of life. So to respond in faith is to take him at his word, to live my life with all my chips gambled on the conviction that he is trustworthy and true. And his trustwor-thiness lies in the truth of his promise and words to us, in who he is and what he does. Most particularly that he is alive for us, present to us, near us. Of course, many refuse to exercise such trust. And there are numerous things which mitigate and oppose true faith. I am going to draw out a couple of them which seem most prevalent in the circles I inhabit; fear and magic.

It seems that fear and anxiety are more prevalent in the water than fluoride. You will know that in your own life, for your family, and in the lives of those you seek to minister to. When we are born we fear being left alone. When we are children we fear not fitting in. When we are teenagers, we fear no one could really know us and love us. Then we fear we might not meet anyone, and even if we do, we fear we, or they, might mess it up. We fear we might not get a job, and then when we get one, we fear we aren't doing it properly. We fear for our own health and the health of others close to us. We fear not having enough and having too much. We fear for our children and their safety, and for their future. We fear being insignificant and expendable. We fear what we are doing to this world. We fear we are missing it. We fear what will become of us. We fear our deaths. And most days of this life, we fear that we are insignificant and unacceptable, self-talk which instils in us an attitude towards ourselves that can most accurately be described as self-hatred. And those are just the big ones. I haven't even mentioned the fact that I didn't get my vehicle tax disc paperwork in on time. If I left the next half of the page empty and asked you to fill it up with your fears and anxieties you'd need more space.

Talking of space, we know anxiety shrinks us. Fear reduces us, holds us back and keeps us captive. Bishop Tom Wright writes in *Following Jesus* that some of the best news of the gospel is that time and time again God commands his people, 'Do not be afraid', 'Do not fear'. (There are over 365 of these commands throughout scripture, more than enough for one for each day of the year.) It's brilliant news. The only trouble is, we haven't got a clue of how to obey it, how to receive it, or how we might act on it.

In the talk I heard you give, Eddie, you pointed out the only thing that Jesus showed disappointment within his ministry was the lack of faith that people had. True. But in many of the references, he rebukes his followers for their lack of faith because they worry and fear. He instructs us to look at the birds, the flowers, the way all creation is provided for. Worry and fear, anxiety and dismay shrink us. And particularly they shrink our faith. Fear is the greatest challenge to trusting.

Now, I used to think that our fear was wrong because those things we feared just weren't going to happen. But that obviously won't do. You and I know that the most crushing thing for some of us is that our greatest fears actually do happen. Jesus doesn't invite us not to fear because with him it's all going to be plain sailing. Faith isn't some kind of get-out-of-jail-free card which exempts the faith-full from the very things we fear.

Rather, we need not be afraid because God is with us; we are not alone, but in the presence of one who is alive to us and for us. The one called Jesus is with us. So to put it bluntly, Eddie, what if the challenge of faith God was giving you as your father was dying was to trust the presence and love and eternal kindness of the Alpha and Omega, who once was dead and is now alive, in the middle of a desperate situation?

The other thing that undermines true faith is magic. It's a subject Henri Nouwen writes profoundly on in *Making All Things New*. Personally I reckon Disney has a lion-king's share of the blame, but I do not have the time or the lawyer to back that up.

When I first moved to London my friend Mel kindly asked me round to hers, with some of her friends, for what she called 'supps'. I think she meant supper, a meal my brother insists on calling tea and other people call dinner. Everyone arrived at her huge flat and most people chit-chatted in the sitting room. Mel was fussing around getting people drinks and announcing in a hopeful voice that the food would be ready 'soon'. I went to see if there was anything I could do to help and arrived in the kitchen to see Mel placing her palms on the glass bit of the oven.

'Chrissy,' (you can probably even imagine her hairstyle) 'it's a nightmare. The potatoes aren't cooked and everything else is.'

'Oh, OK. So what are you doing?'

'I'm laying hands on the oven and praying they would be cooked.'

'You're kidding.'

'No. And if you're a man of faith, you'll come over here and help me out.'

I backed towards the door.

'OK then, I'll do it on my own.'

She deliberately placed her hands once again on the oven door, looked intently through the smoky-burnt glass and spoke to the potatoes, 'In the name of Jesus … *be cooked.*'

I turned to leave.

'Aren't you going to see if it worked?' Mel shouted after me.

'Mel, if that worked, I'm giving up the faith.'

Wonderfully, miraculously, the potatoes were as hard as stones.

Where does magic come into this, you might ask? Let me explain. If I understood it right, your conviction of needing to have more faith betrayed your assumption that if enough faith could be summoned and mustered and wrestled onto the divine scales, they might tip in favour of something miraculous happening for your dad. For me this makes faith something like a magical ingredient in a situation. And I get squeamish that speaking words of faith and acting on them could tip over into feeling a bit like spells and superstition. So we need to get our balancing pole out as we navigate this tightrope.

My mate Mark goes each month to a prayer meeting for Patrick, a friend who is chronically and progressively ill with a condition that constantly threatens his life. Patrick's wonderful friends have been meeting for years now, praying for his health, his recovery and his healing. A few months ago, a couple of others came to the group. Frustrated that Patrick didn't seem to be getting better, they suggested that the reason for this was his lack of faith. A winning combination – not only has he got a condition that is chronic and life-threatening, but it is his own lack of faith which keeps him from being healed. Fortunately those that suggested this were booted out of the prayer meeting.

Just yesterday on the interweb I watched a talk by a flavour-of-the-year speaker who rounded on us listeners for being the reason we didn't see more miracles. It was our lack of faith. This is not the first time I have been the weak link in the chain of God bringing complete transformation to the nation. I remember first meeting you at a prayer meeting on a gloriously sunny day eight years ago in the football ground here in Reading. We were told that if we truly believed, it would mark the start of nationwide revival. Is it just my fault that it didn't? But I will ride my residual guilt and claim I really can't be doing with this faith-as-the-magic-ingredient kind of thing.

When I was eight years old I went to see Notts County Football Club play at every home game. The first game I went to was goalless for ages until I decided to sit on my match day programme. At that moment my team scored. From then on I sat on my programme throughout every match. It never worked again, but it didn't stop me trying. Too often faith is held out as the magic ingredient. Some even have magic words and techniques to go along with it. On the fringes of the Christian faith there have always been those who claim they have had some exclusive revelation of some special techniques to get nearer, closer, more powerfully in God's zone. They are called gnostics and from the earliest days were known as heretics. They are always worth avoiding. Can faith really be about willing ourselves to believe things that are sublimely unbelievable, which if we can unflinchingly declare and be confident of, will bring about the miraculous? I think not.

However, I know that such a position can easily tip into a listless apathy and cynicism, in which faith makes no iota of difference, and our attitude to life becomes a fatalistic *que sera sera*, whatever will be. No. Faith makes all the difference. God is not a word for what is already happening (a great line, I know – not mine but from Walter Brueggemann's *Prophetic Imagination*).

Faith, as I said earlier, makes me get on the bus. We act faith out. Trust brings change, it makes a difference to what we hold out for. Faith is anything but passive. Faith expects. But it's God's presence that brings this change, not the presence of my faith. Faith creates the conditions for it, if you like. It's not a magic ingredient – but it is a holding out on God to do miraculous things. I love the way David Ford talks about it in *The Shape of Living*, one of the best books written in the 1990s:

… the longing is for something magical, a quick fix, the miraculous touch or medicine, the dramatic release. And occasionally the miracle does happen. One of the best attested facts is that he healed people. God is a God of surprises, hears prayers and has compassion on suffering. It is always right to ask.

But it is clear too that prayer is not magic or a slot machine. God is not a God of quick fixes and easy instantaneous solutions … God is above all concerned with love and long-term faithfulness, with healing hearts, minds and communities as well as bodies.

So, to be totally specific to you Eddie, in the situation you found yourself in with your dad; yes God could bring healing, but faith is a trust that God is there in the healing or in the dying. Faith does not believe God is only present when death is put off. Faith is not the rubbing of the genie's lamp. Faith is rather an active, radical, trust in God. But here's why and how should we trust him.

We trust this God because of Jesus. He is the one who holds out to us the gift of faith, saying something like: 'Dare to believe that despite yourself, God is for you, he loves you and acts to welcome, forgive and restore you, to use you and bring his hope to his world.' It is he who creates the capacity for faith. Time and time again in his earthly life the words he spoke and the things he did called out trust and faith in people. It was radical trust and faith. It made people switch their jobs and sell their possessions, it made people lower friends down through strangers' roofs and inspired women to touch the hem of his garment. These people were responding to the faith they had received from the words and works of Jesus. Amongst the most unlikely of people – sex workers, gamblers, fraudsters and shifty outcasts – the words, stories and actions of Jesus held out the achingly beautiful reality that they were loved and accepted by the God who made them. And they responded with faith. Jesus tells us we are loved, accepted and delighted in. It is not about our capacities or capabilities. Without any possibility on our side, God's great possibility comes into view. What he tells us of himself and his great love for us in inaccessible and inconceivable to us; we are loved. It is truly miraculous. And it's unbelievable only in the sense that it feels too good to be true. The theologian Paul Tillich, who wasn't given to sentimentalism, said that faith is the courage to accept acceptance.

To those around Jesus, faith was a response to what they met in him. Faith is the great 'yes'; not only a yes to the words he has spoken, but to the one speaking them. The gift is determined by the one in whom we have faith. – as Eugene Peterson writes in *The Jesus Way*:

> The fatal thing is to reduce faith to an explanation. It is not an explanation. It is a passion.

I have maybe spent too long in this letter saying what I think faith isn't. As well as saying it is receiving the gift of God's trustworthy presence, let me set out the conditions faith might best thrive in.

One of the things we tend to do with many of the central tenets of Christianity is to individualise and privatise them. It becomes all about me. So with faith, it becomes about my faith. Now, of course, there is something intensely personal and significant for me in the shape and state of my personal trusting relationship with God. But the tragedy is, we are less than used to practising it together. Kierkegaard uses a great analogy for this in his book *Provocations*:

> Imagine a violinist. If, without having learned the least bit of music, he were to take his seat in the orchestra and right away begin playing, he would not only be disturbed but would disturb others. No, for a long time he practises by himself, alone. As far as possible not a thing disturbs him there; he sits and beats time but his aim is to play in the orchestra. He must be able to tolerate the profusion of the most varied instruments, this interweaving of sounds, and yet be able to attend to

his violin and play along just as calmly and confidently as if he were home alone in his room. Oh this again makes is necessary for him to be by himself to learn to be able to do this – but the aim is always that he play in the orchestra. It is the same with faith and the task of living it out.

Faith is personal (a better word than individual) and corporate. My experience testifies that if I am not alive to God on my own, I will be less alive to God in a corporate gathering. If I am not praying alone, I will not really engage with prayer in a wider setting. Faith is formed not simply in the seismic moments which will define my life, but in the disciplines and desires that I foster day after day. Yet it is with others that I stand and sit and kneel and bow, finding my place with the other faith-full. As someone involved in leadership you will be familiar with the conversations in which people confess to feeling that their faith is weak and flimsy. My reply to such confessions is that it's not their faith, it's ours. And if they are finding it tough, they can ride on the coat tails of the rest of us for a bit.

I think the thing that particularly stirs us about the Peter story, and the line which says how well he did getting out of the boat, is that we know faith demands things from us. We want our faith to change our actions. On this Pete Rollins, writing in *How (Not to) Speak of God*, is surely right:

> I recently heard a well known speaker say that if faith does not cost us something then it is nothing. Only much later could I respond: if faith does not cost us everything, it is nothing.

My take is that staying in the boat and trusting would have taken more faith than getting over the side. But our sense that faith demands something from us is one we can trust. Our modern-day patriarch, Rowan Williams, says in *Tokens of Trust*:

> Don't imagine the Bible is full of comfortable and reassuring things about the life of belief and trust; it

isn't. It is often about the appalling cost of letting God come near you and of trying to trust him when all the evidence seems to have gone.

Faith requires constant challenge and honing, re-orientating and weighing, and of course we cannot be trusted to test ourselves. That would create our own monsters. But despite what we might choose, we know that suffering hones and refines us. Kierkegaard again: 'Adversities do not make people weak – they reveal what strength they actually have.'

It's in this troubled crucible that we see faith purified. Is it just me, but when a grieving mother talks of forgiving the gang members who have murdered her son, is that not faith-inspiring? When a Rwandan Tutsi woman stands before the Hutu soldier who raped her and murdered her children, and yet can hold out a hand of peace, is that not truly faith-building? When parents tell of trusting God even though their only child died in a random tragedy, is that not the real deal? This does it for me in the realm of faith, far more than shiny, glitzy stories.

The place in the Old Testament where the audacious require-ment of faith is most brutally seen is with Abraham. This story is one of the reasons why Abraham is known as a hero of faith, and features in the wonderful Hebrews 11 roll of honour. It's a story which would necessitate a public enquiry today. Abraham is told by God to take Isaac, his only son to Mount Moriah, where he must sacrifice him. Three times Abraham is addressed and he answers and obeys. You'll remember that Isaac is the son born to Abraham and Sarah in their old age; he is the child of the promise, the one who fulfils the covenant, through whom all people on earth would be blessed. God is bringing a future out of something that this old, infertile couple, Abraham and Sarah, had no power to create. It's this child of the promise who is the focus for the test. And the test is very basic; for Abraham to go and sacrifice his son. But the reason for the test is not.

It could be that God just wants to see if Abraham will do what he says; a how-much-power-do-I-have-over-this-one? It could be that God wants to know if Abraham trusts God will keep his promise about his family blessing the whole world even if Isaac isn't alive. Or it could be that God wants to test where Abraham's faith truly lies. I have no time for number one, and lean towards the second two. Here's why.

I wonder if the following has happened; Isaac has been born, he is the gift, the laugh, the miracle child, the one who will be the fulfilment of the promise and vocation of this family. And this wonderful miracle son has become the doted-on hinge of the future, the fulfilment, the one in who all the hopes and fears are held, who all the poker chips have been staked on. That is, he has become an idol. Idols are usually good things, given as gifts, which then take too high a place. Loaded with a significance and prominence they were never made for, and which they are unable to healthily bear, they start to dehumanise us and the processes we put around them.

So this test is actually about who Abraham is prepared to put at the centre of his life. Who is the one he will make the decisions around? This is a God who asks for everything. Faith, for Abraham in this regard, is not a matter of commitment to some vague principles of being kind and good; this is not some God of balance and reasonableness. This is a God who is uncompromising in his request. Abraham chooses to respond in faith by orientating his life around God, rather than simply his gifts, even though this gift was essential to him fulfilling his vocation.

So Abraham loads the wood onto his own son and they set out for the mountain of sacrifice. Isaac seems to be unaware of what is going on, and asks his father where the sacrifice is. 'God himself will provide the sacrifice,' says Abraham. They carry on and eventually arrive at the top of the hill. Abraham makes the altar and ties up his son, taking the knife in his hand. He is about to deliver the fatal blow when God calls to him. Fortunately he hears. 'Don't hurt the boy,' God says. Then Abraham sees a ram caught in a thick thorn bush. They take the ram and kill it, and so call the place 'The Lord will provide'. They then go down the hill. I wonder what they talked about on the way down?

In this painful and, to our modern ears, rather toe-curling narrative there are huge challenges on the theme of faith. What might be your and my Isaac? Are we willing to give up, to sacrifice our idols on this altar? But I find myself ending up not thinking about Abraham or poor Isaac at all. For they don't go through with the sacrifice. Because God himself provided the sacrifice.

What is enacted on Mount Moriah by Abraham and Isaac is brought to fulfilment generations later on the same spot. Mount Moriah is actually located just outside of Jerusalem. We know it better as Golgotha. And here we see not a ram caught in thorns, but a lamb wearing a crown of thorns. There a son, an only son, the son of promise, the one through whom this vocation to all people will be fulfilled, and he, joined by two others, carries the wood he will be sacrificed upon through the streets that have been built since Isaac took his.

And we get to the crux of faith.

One of the biggest privileges in my life is to be around people as they die, although that probably romanticises it too much. But there have been times around death that I have been aware of being in those thin places between heaven and earth.

At exactly the same time I heard you talk of your father being admitted to the hospice, one of my best friends' mother was dying. She knew it was going to come, and she prepared herself and her son for it. She did it with characteristic dignity and aplomb. On Christmas Eve, less than two months before she died, we sat and talked, or rather I tried to say nothing, and just listen to this woman who knew this was going to be the last Christmas with her beloved son and his family. She was riding into death with her eyes wide open and her arms extended. She was full of hope. Not for healing, but for God.

By January she was in hospital and I went to visit her again. This time there was no sense of peace in the room. She had received a visitor who had told her that she could, no she must, hold on to God for healing. She talked about this not in ways which revealed this as something she wanted, but in ways which showed she felt she was letting everyone down if she didn't believe it. Then she asked if I believed it, and if she did die, whether we would all pray for her to be resurrected. Because, she had been told, this would be a wonderful example of faith and testimony to others.

Gently, gently we prised these foreign objects from her hands. It was not hard for her to lay them down as they were so alien to her. She never spoke like that again; instead she faced full on the death that was on the horizon. She died some weeks later.

My questions are for those who went to her and made it sound, even if unwittingly, that to be faith-full at such a point in her life would be to believe for healing or resurrection. What is it about death that those of us who follow the one who was dead but is now alive again, are so afraid of? Faith faces death with hope. Faith isn't seen in ducking death, but in facing it. Death is the litmus test for hope. In death faith comes alive.

My deepest conviction is that hundreds of years later, on this Mount of Moriah that was Golgotha, the ultimate act of faith is shown. For here one who, like Abraham, had wrestled in Gethsemane at what was being asked of him, went through the ultimate sacrifice, and faced his own death.

Jesus had lived his whole life for the God he called Father. He had taught for him, healed for him, proclaimed his kingdom and flung open its gates to invite all in. He had proclaimed grace to all in his words and deeds. He had talked of him being caring and trustworthy, of him knowing the hairs on our heads and caring for us like the ultimate parent. Everything in his life had been orientated around serving and loving this God. Yet it was his firm belief that what God required from him was to lay down his life. He faced his fears and anxieties and trusted. His faith in God demands the most radical action.

For here he hung on a cross. From his cry it was clear he felt utterly isolated and desolate. He had no definites about his life, his death or what might be beyond that. He simply trusted the one for whom he had lived.

I suggest that, 'Father into your hands I commend my spirit', is the ultimate confession of faith. In this moment, as in the whole of his life, he referred everything to his Father. Staring into the abyss, with the forces of hell coming against him, he trusted the relentless love of the one he had lived for and died for. A father who this time was called on to sacrifice his only son; yet this only son was not some passive victim, but chose it every step of the way. The same angels who were around to stop Abraham seemed to be around Jesus, as he told one dying beside him he could have called ten thousand angels to stop it all.

But unlike what they did for Abraham, the angels didn't stop the sacrifice. God never asks anything of us that he hasn't done himself. The faith that is held out to us, that we are invited into, offered, commanded to, is faith that has been tried and tested. It is a faith which faces death and trusts. It is a faith which stakes everything on the love that is shown us by the one who gave himself up for us. It is the hope of a faith that shows itself to be true in death and in seismic, *ex nihilo*, resurrection future. Death with Jesus is never the last word. This must never be underestimated.

As C. S. Lewis wrote in *The Screwtape Letters* when he put these words into the mouth of Screwtape, the senior devil, giving advice to his younger nephew Wormwood:

> Do not be deceived, Wormwood; our cause [that is the Devil's cause] is never more in danger than when a human, no longer desiring, but still intending, to do the enemy's will [that is, God's will], looks around upon a universe from which every trace of him seems to have vanished, and asks why he has been forsaken, and still obeys.

Eddie, faith is God's gift to you. It is inspired by him, summoned up by him, held out by him. We simply bring our open hands and hearts to receive it. There are times when we hold onto it for dear life. Time after time things in us militate against it – fear, desire for the painless quick fix – but amongst the faith-full, and in the middle of this life, even in those things we would never choose to happen, we sense a stronger-than-death trust rising in us. But faith is a trusting response to the word held out to us in Jesus; that God is with us, that death can be faced without terrible fear, and that because this one was dead but now is alive again, that love is stronger than hatred, light is stronger than darkness, good will triumph over evil, truth will unmask the lies, that nothing can separate us from the love of Christ.

That is why week after week God's inspired and weak people, his faltering and faith-full people, his sinking and trusting serv-ants, his stubborn and strong children, his broken and hopeful friends meet around his table and celebrate his faithfulness in bread and wine. Here, around this table the contingency of life is faced. We remember that within twenty-four hours of this meal being given the host was dead. None of us knows what this next week might hold. But we do know we are held in the hands of a God who is ultimately trustworthy with our lives: our hopes, our fears, our loved ones, our deaths. And we entrust ourselves into his most faithful presence and love.

Eddie, your faith in Jesus is obvious. Your father did not die because you didn't have enough faith to believe his cancer-riddled body could be miraculously cured. Your father died because he had cancer and something will get us all in the end. Faith trusts that even in the middle of such storms, the one who was dead and is alive again is present, can be trusted and hoped in, and will eventually bring us safely to his new shore.

Stay in the boat,

Chris

3

Belonging

To Anthonia

Aunty Ant is the world's greatest aunty. Nothing makes my daughters more excited than her arrival. She is a wonderful person. Everyone knows it. She comes to stay with us every third weekend and always leaves before our church service starts. It's as if she has a repellent in her for the corporate.

Aunty Ant is solid in her Christian faith. She would go to the stake for it. It's in the marrow of her bones. Sometimes I say things which cause her to give me one of those 'Please don't knock my precarious stack of faith over' looks, and I do this without even trying to be controversial. It happens when I say things like: 'Of course dinosaurs lived, Hope,' or: 'I don't know whether Noah's flood covered the whole of the earth, Jessie,' or: 'Yes, Dora, because of what Jesus did your friend Muhammad might well be in heaven.'

Anthonia loves God and believes everything in the Bible in a way that I don't. But she doesn't care for church. And so she never goes. She used to with the family as a teenager, to a church that some still regard as epoch-making in its legacy. So she has tasted it, and maybe she can't bring herself to be let down by inferior models, or maybe she just thinks she can do without.

It's not simply that I think she might be missing out, that belonging to a church might give her something else to be involved in, or that it would be Good for Her. It's because she must.

Dear Anthonia,

I was thinking of starting this by saying that this was a copy of a sermon I preached at church and as you had missed it I thought I'd send it to you. But that would be a lie, and nothing I want to set out to you about belonging to church is based on lies. In fact, I feel so strongly about it because of truth. What I want to do is to try to convince you of the necessity for church, not in the abstract but in real life.

This is what I'm going to try to do in this letter; first I am going to try to set out what's at stake, and what is at the heart of the existence of church – the Why? Where? What? and Who? of church. Then I will lay out the framework of worship, time and a physical location as the coordinates that the life of any and every church best plots itself to live within. Having tried to get some clarity there, I will explain the tasks that I think should be closest to the heart of the church, and look at how we might all, together, go about fulfilling them.

You always say how grateful you are that you didn't know me when I was younger, in my (even more) opinionated days. I know, the mind boggles, doesn't it? In fact, all I can remember from my post-graduate seminars at Cambridge is how very clever and opinionated everyone else was. This was usually exhibited by them asking questions I couldn't even understand, yet alone work out an answer to. But the best question was one I could understand, and it was asked by Tiffany. I think you'd have liked her. She had done an architecture degree and was now combining this with some theology by researching the question 'Can church buildings be heretical?' At the heart of this was the suggestion that church buildings in their physical layout and make-up could contradict the very faith they stood for.

Now this question might not interest you, in and of itself (if it does, read *Flickering Pixels* by Shane Hipps), but let's take it wider and say it's not just about buildings; what if we consider whether the church itself might not contradict the very faith it lives by and for? What would a church look like that truly lived the faith?

This isn't a take-it-or-leave-it question, because I will throw the gauntlet down now – there should be no such thing as churchless Christianity. To seek to live Christian faith on your own is to pursue something that contradicts the very thing Christianity is about. Church is about the kind of God that God is. What I want to do is set out to you why I think church is non-negotiable.

One of the writers I love reading the most is Eugene Peterson. He was involved in leading the same congregation for more than twenty-five years. You'd have thought such a stretch would have made him rather church-weary. Instead, in his book *Christ Plays in Ten Thousand Places* he says this:

> There can be no maturity in the spiritual life, no obedience in following Jesus, no wholeness in the Christian life, apart from an immersion and embrace of community. I am not myself by myself. Community, not the highly vaunted individualism of our culture, is the setting in which Christ is at play.

'Church' comes from the Greek word *ekklesia*, which means gathering together. It's something we do before it's something that describes what we are; it's a verb before it's a noun. But why is this gathering of people so vital?

It's so vital because of truth. The thing is, I really don't want to bludgeon you into going to church, to guilt-trip you into it, or to bribe you into it by over-selling. I want to truth you into church.

The truth isn't just that we are made to exist in community; the truth isn't just that we need one another; the truth isn't just that we are stronger together, or can't do it alone. The truth is that God made us for this and calls us into this, primarily for God, then for us, and then for God's world.

The theologian Stanley Hauerwas (who was voted the 'Best Theologian' in the United States recently and, when asked to comment, said the category of 'best' wasn't a Christian one – so you know we're going to love him) is even more polemic than Peterson. In his book *Resident Aliens* he says:

> The most interesting, creative, political solutions we
> Christians have to offer our troubled society are not
> new laws, advice to politicians, or increased funding of
> social programmes. The most creative social strategy we
> have to offer is the church.

But again to be back-to-basics clear; we are not talking ideals
here. We are talking reality.

I know that for you any whiff of being over-optimistic will,
quite rightly, cause you to put this letter aside. So from the outset
I want to honour the good things you experienced in church
some years ago, but hold out an olive branch that the best may be
still to come. But that is not because I will be romantic about
church. In fact the only people who ever are are those who
haven't truly been part of one. The New Testament never presents
a congregation apart from its problems. The things we face now
are the things Christian communities have always faced: strong
characters pulling in different directions, questions of theology,
sex, who's in and who's out, divisions, not getting on, the people
who wind us up, money, who to listen to, how we relate to
authority, our attitude to the world around us, drink, helping the
poor, racism, suffering and the question of where on earth Jesus
has got to in all this. In dealing with church we aren't dealing
with a model community in imaginary conditions. We are
dealing with who we are and where we are now. While there is a
universal nature of church (this is the catholicity that the creeds
refer to) church never exists in the abstract but in the particular,
the specific, the identifiable.

My opening salvo on where to start to lay out a vision of
church before you is that the Why? How? What? and Who? of
church are answered in one word; God.

The church is, because God is. We are part of this body
because we are invited by a God whose work begins it all.
Church is the response, called into being as a faithful witness to
who he is and what he has done.

Once again this is not just any concept of God. You work in a
highly pressurised environment with those who do not share

your faith. You know from conversations over the panini grill that there are as many different concepts of God as there are people. But the Christian faith champions that God reveals himself through Jesus as Father, Son and Spirit, three in one, united in a relationship of mutual service, delight and love. Just as this God's very being is in relationship, so, as those who bear his image, is ours. Because the life of God is communal, so is our life. The church has been described as an echo of God's divine life, as a mini-fractal patterning his own life. This God calls us into life together. Church is his. If you ever hear a church leader talk of 'my church', correct them, because it's embarrassingly revealing about their ego and more importantly, and slightly less embarrassingly maybe, it's not true. It's God's church.

We enter into this life together publicly in baptism. Here, with varying quantities of water and ceremony (I have never quite got over the fact that the Desert Fathers baptised in spit), since the earliest days of the church, those who sense the call of God to join his church are renamed by the Father, the Son and the Holy Spirit. You'll remember when the girls were baptised that the rhetoric is soaring in describing what is going on. This is where each person's ministry begins; this is where our incorporation in the divine life of God is celebrated.

In *Christ Plays in Ten Thousand Places* Peterson pleads:

> If you want to know who I am and what makes me tick, don't for heaven's sake look up my IQ or give me a Myers-Briggs profile … but set me in the company of the Father, Son and the Holy Spirit.

Being part of this body isn't just an option for the extroverts or for those who have a bit more time on their hands. Church isn't a best idea, an ideal for those who are fortunate to live close to a functional one. It is a truth in and of itself. When we follow Jesus we are part of it. We can live as if it's not the case, but we are all an essential part of this. God speaks first and has spoken us into being. Belonging is essentially obedience to the summons of

God; that in Christ we are summoned by the Father, into this community that lives by the Spirit.

But that's all quite big a picture and I know you'll want some details of history.

Back in the book we have more discussion about than any other, Genesis, you might remember that in chapter 12, God brings a people into being (Israel) and does great things for them and through them. If you have a ruler you can draw some fairly strong lines from God's choice in the Old Testament of a people who will be his light in the world and through whom all nations of the earth will be blessed, to the language that is used for the church, for example by Peter, in the New Testament. That Jesus chooses twelve disciples obviously isn't haphazard, as if he would ideally have liked fifteen but could only find twelve; he is recreating the twelve tribes of Israel around himself. My take is that God's people, Israel, took their chosenness as them being more special, but they were chosen to tell the rest of the world God had chosen them too. God works through the particular for the universal. Israel failed to live their vocation. Jesus took it on, lived it, died doing it, and then passed it through his breath into his followers. (Obviously the relationship of the church to the chosen people is a highly controversial issue – I'm a great fan of all N. T. Wright has to say on this, for example in *The New Testament and the People of God*.)

The language of the New Testament for the church uses all these ancient and loaded phrases:

> But you are a chosen people, a royal priesthood, a holy nation, God's special possession, that you may declare the praises of him who called you out of darkness into his wonderful light. Once you were not a people, but now you are the people of God; once you had not received mercy, but now you have received mercy.
>
> (*1 Peter 2:9–10*)

The church is in existence because Jesus calls a people into existence, who would not be, if he hadn't called them. And the call comes not as some generous offer (although it is), not as some life-enhancing choice (although it is). He calls us into being because he is Christ, the Lord or *Kurios* (it's a first-century political title for a ruler who laid claim to divine authority). We are creatures of this Lord, and he bids us follow him. Jesus doesn't stand for office, he doesn't campaign for our vote, he doesn't seek our endorsement. He isn't selling a product, or trying to get more supporters. He summons us to follow him, not alone but together, right into the heart of the divine life.

It's possible to respond to him because of the Spirit. The Spirit enables us to hear him and obey him, to take and to trust his outstretched hand to us. And when this Spirit breathes on us we come to life together, and a body is once again conceived. The Spirit that brought life to conceive Jesus of Nazareth's body in the womb of Mary brings his life to a random group of individuals to enflesh, to tabernacle, to incarnate himself once again in his world. The church is, then, the Body of Christ. The first Christians, who used these words to describe the church, knew what it was like to be around the physical body of Jesus of Nazareth. Now they are using the Body of Christ language to describe the community that gathers in his name because it feels as if he is around again.

God is always present to his world. The reason those beautiful trees in your parents' garden stay up, that the oceans swell, that the world revolves and the planets orbit is because God is present to his world. But in Jesus, God the eternal Son was present in flesh, concentrate if you like, in the very body of Jesus of Nazareth. So now, God is present to his world, upholding, sustaining, creating, loving. But he is especially present, uniquely present, in his Body, the church.

We had one conversation some years ago when you had read somewhere that the word Christian means 'Little Christ'. I think I might have been too polite about what I think about such talk. So to be clear: No. No, it doesn't. And it never has. On so many levels this is wrong and dangerous. It's hard enough to be ourselves let alone to be Jesus. It's a nice phrase for a bookmark, but the old: 'Jesus has no hands but our hands, no feet but our feet', is just plain wrong. Jesus does have hands, and feet, and eyes and ears, for he is in heaven, where he lives and prays for us. I just can't get 'Jesus' language for individuals. But I am compelled to use 'Jesus' language for ourselves corporately – we together are his hands in this world, we together are his feet, together show his heart; communally we show his love. If you want to know where God is in the world, in the concrete, in the specific, in the particular, be part of God's church.

Now I know it doesn't always feel like this. In fact let's be honest, it sometimes doesn't feel like this because it isn't the case. I know there are lots of churchless Christians; we also know there is such a thing as a Christianless church. The church must continually orientate and re-orientate its life around the God who called it into being. You can contradict the very thing you stand for. As a fine old man called Reinhold Niebuhr once asked, 'Why is it that so many Christians look like those stars who are advertising products you know they aren't using themselves?'

Worship is the orientation of life around God. It's a response to the love of God which has addressed us, captured us, brought us into being and given us hope. The church is not anything as banal as a museum of information about God, defenders of ancient doctrines or beliefs, but the people who experience him, who know him as present to them. It's God's presence that is cherished, celebrated and desired above all else. A church's primary responsibility is to be alive to God. When I arrived at St Laurence I found a small congregation of eleven people who met week by week for a sung eucharist. They did it brilliantly, with polished and perfected performances. The trouble was that their familiarity with church, even these holy things, had inoculated them against the very thing itself; they had become stale to God. This is true in every tradition.

The *ekklesia* is the gathered body who meet to encounter God. This has been done week in week out, in song and psalms, in listening to scripture and prayer, in confessing sins and breaking bread and sharing wine. There is a content in what Christians do when they gather together that makes it church. But the form that content takes differs from congregation to congregation, dependent on who we are, what our culture is and what God is doing among us at this time. Many of us are giving our best years to trying to forge what a church in and for this culture might look like. While we want to honour and respect the tradition of the Christian faith, we are not convinced just rolling along in the same way that we've always done is what we are called to. Call it emerging if you like, call it fresh, call it doing church differently. Personally, I just call it church.

At St Laurence we have been at this for some eleven years now. A couple of years in we were tying ourselves in knots about how we could enable the young people who were coming to faith to engage with God in a way that was authentic to them. Things changed when one of our young adults said, 'Do you know what … when young people come to faith they will know how to worship, they will know how to pray.' It's only then that I realised what rubbish it was to expect young people to be able to know instinctively how to do these things. That's like saying our girls know what food is best for them. No, rather it is the church's job to teach people how to connect with God, how to worship, how to pray in Jesus' name, how to hear God in Scripture. And we do that best living by God's rhythm.

One of the major ways in which you'll find the church doing this is by living in God's time, by his calendar and not our own. Your year revolves round big events – family birthdays and celebrations, ski-ing, Wimbledon and *The Apprentice*. Along with the seasons, these events shape your year. And the church lives a year. This helps us with our orientation around God, and it gifts us with a sense of God's timing.

It takes time to be a Christian. Some things may make sense quickly, others take far longer. My professor at Cambridge, David Ford, used to encourage people who wanted to commit to following Jesus, to commit to do it for at least a year, so as to live in God's time. We all feel time is the most precious commodity we have in these impatient days of our lives. But God gives time more generously and spaciously, more profoundly and patiently than we do. The church pattern of living in God's time looks a bit like this:

Advent: a season of looking forward to the return of Jesus to wrap up history as we know it. A time of hope and judgement, of weighing our lives in the balance of eternity.
Key themes: watching, waiting, expecting, imagining.

Christmas: a celebration of the incarnation, of the mystery of God taking flesh, God with us.
Key themes: joy, wonder, love and delight.

Epiphany: the showing of God, his presence in our lives, his revelation of himself to us.
Key themes: Listening, marking, committing.

Lent: begun on Ash Wednesday, a time of self-reflection and discipline, of considering how our own discipleship is going and shaping our lives on the choices of Jesus.
Key themes: repentance, facing the truth, rigour, honesty.

Holy Week and Good Friday: considering the story of Jesus' passion; his choices and our choices, his character and the themes of life and death, love and hatred, commitment and betrayal enacted in the drama of these events.
Key themes: betrayal, suffering, pain, god-forsakenness, death.

Easter: the unexpected life that God brings from nothing; his new resurrection life dawning and let loose on the old world.
Key themes: surprise, hope, light, praise, expectation, a thousand new starts.

Pentecost: the breath of Jesus coming to bring his people into existence, to draw them into the rhythm of his life and love, and to equip them for being God's faithful witnesses in his world.
Key themes: empowering, gifts, need, community.

If we live this Christian year, we live every emotion and incident of our own story, but each one is addressed in the context of God's great story in Jesus. There are highs and lows, up times and down times, intense times and spacious times. We do not attempt to live on a constant high.

I used to attend a church in which the prayer every week would be that the 'meeting' ('services' were off trend) would be one which would change our lives. Now I can do that for a couple of weeks, but not for fifty-two weeks a year. It's exhausting. If this is the requirement, we will just burn out or create artificial highs. No, we live feast days and fast days, holy days and ordinary time. Not every gathering changes our lives, but we live in the rhythm of the God who does.

I think you once told me that more people die in the desert of drowning than of dehydration. This is because they camp in the wadi in the hope of being near the water. But when the flash floods come they sweep everything away. Some churches have set up camp in the wadis because they are waiting for the next flood of water. It stops them moving on. They need to just journey with God. As if that's easy. But it highlights being alive to God. We need to be wide awake to how God is with us and how he calls to be with each other.

Enter the Bible. This is not some little instruction book for our individual life; not some kind of provider of a cross-reference for today's problem. These scriptures provide a map of the terrain, stories for the journey and a sense of thrill our search for the destination. Church history provides us with wonderful examples and faithful inspiration in living it, and resources to keep us alive on our journey.

The church you talk more about than any other is the one you were part of with your family during the 1980s. I have heard you say it was like the church would have been in the New Testament. The trouble is, we get a bit dewy-eyed about those churches. When I hear people talk of 'just going back to being a New Testament church' I wonder if they really mean it. What with all the splits (Galatia), the drunkenness (Corinth), the incest (Corinth) and the pride (Philippi)? No, such idealising of the picture of church in the New Testament does none of us any good. We need a healthy reading of our history. And in humility to bear in mind Archbishop Rowan William's comment in his keynote address at the Fresh Expressions conference *Changing the Landscape*: 'For all we know we still are the early church.' Today there are wonderful pioneers and communities exploring new frontiers. But there is no model that can just be transposed to where we are now.

Last year, I heard that Subway had become the largest fast food outlet in the UK. We have seven now in Reading. Dan tells me the 7-inch breakfast sub is great. Subway has expanded because it is a franchise – every branch does everything the same. They have the same uniforms, the same food, the same preparation, the same menu, the same offers, the same décor. You could open one today. Although I am not suggesting you do, and certainly not in Reading.

Some churches seek to plant franchise churches where you just open a new outlet and do everything the same; same uniform, same songs, same décor, same message, same courses, same strategy, same chips. At its best, what's behind it is a desire to reproduce a successful model, something that has 'worked'. And at worst it betrays wonky theology about the church. There are no easy answers, no just-add-boiling water solutions. The trouble is, and I speak as someone in church leadership, there are days, no months, when I would love there to be some magic answer.

But all that takes me away from being alive to what is going on with us and God. Picture this. It's a lovely summer's day and you are walking through Sulham Woods, you know, the ones fifteen minutes away from here. There are various trees on either side of the path. There is nothing else to look at so you start taking an interest in each particular tree. You see one that looks as if it has the lushest green leaves on it, so you go and take a closer look. As you get closer you realise that the green leaves belong to ivy that has grown around the actual tree. The tree itself has no leaves, no greenery, no signs of life, and what look like its healthy leaves actually come from something apart from its body.

I wonder whether this is an image of what we settle for in our churches. We get the leaves, they are green and from a distance we look alive, but it's all coming from outside – from courses and projects, from schemes and imposed models from other places. But what about the life within? There is always more at stake in the life of the church than merely numbers.

In the novel *Chasing Francis* by Ian Morgan Cron we are introduced to the character Chase Falson. He is the founder of an all singin', all dancin' mega church in New England, USA.

Everything is going from strength to strength until a single woman in his church suffers the death of her daughter. He realises that he has nothing of any depth to say to her. Under instruction from the elders of the church, he takes time away and goes to Assisi to spend time with his uncle who is a Franciscan monk. He is introduced to Saint Francis and this encounter changes everything. When he returns he sets forward the marks of a church he wants to be part of: transcendence, community, beauty, dignity and meaning. And these are all qualities that cannot be imposed from outside. But the enemies of a renewed church come from without. Rowan Williams identified three: entertainment, problem-solving and trying to fit God around the edges of your identity.

> The church's most credible form of witness is the actual creation of a living, breathing, visible community of faith.

Or as Stanley Hauerwas regularly encourages people to grasp, the church is the hermeneutic for the Gospel. That is, people will understand the good news we are talking about when they see how we live it.

Churchless Christianity isn't an option because I cannot follow Jesus on my own. Nor can I be selective of the company of those I journey with. Jesus is not discriminating about his children. Everyone is chosen. This is where being children of our culture most tarnishes us. We are so used to consulting our *Which?* reports and having the ability to choose the perfect option, and we think this can translate into our life with God. Not only does it not transfer over, it militates against us embracing life as it really is. For there are no ideal communities, no hybrid churches, no gathering for people of the same social group, class, taste or social mobility. The conditions in which a life following Jesus can best take is surrounded by different people. Sure, gather with your friends, do social things with those who share your taste and lifestyle choices, but never exclude those who don't do this from coming to church with you. Here in this community the dignity of all is upheld, hospitality is offered to all, the place of all is cherished and the contribution of all is expected. Church isn't about attendance at meetings, it's about belonging to a people.

Back in the day there used to be big discussions about the relationship of Christian faith to church. In terms of faith, it used to be said that people would first start to change how they acted, then change what they believed, and then become part of the church. It was even turned it into a jaunty phrase, 'behave, believe, belong'. Nowadays, people think it's 'belong, believe, behave'; belonging comes before believing, which comes before behaving.

To be honest, it's more like belong, belong, belong. Being part of church means committing to a diverse group of people. And as my friend Jim says, commitment isn't just a declaration, it's a behaviour. Love is never an abstract thing. It's a particular thing. The only people you'll hear talking about community with a misty-eyed romanticism are those who have clearly never been part of one. Nothing can be harder than loving other people. Apart from maybe, opening yourself up to be truly loved – known and not rejected, known more and still not rejected.

But here as the church of Jesus Christ we try to set up a loving community which swims against the tide, which believes that the most dangerous thing in the world is conditional love, and instead pledges to love unconditionally. In community we love and are let down, we are misunderstood and taken for granted, we are undervalued and hurt. But here we learn to listen and put the needs of others before our own, we learn to share and be vulnerable, we learn to give for the sake of what is given rather than what will be given back. Here we learn life's most important lesson; how to love. As David Ford writes in *The Shape of Living:*

> We constantly meet with faces and voices which appeal to us to help, to have compassion or to take some practical responsibility that goes beyond what our commitment or inclinations oblige us to. They pose one of the biggest questions to us and our communities;

> how do we cope with the suffering of the poor, the
> hungry, the impaired, the marginalised, the victim?
> These may be the test of the right shaping of our hearts
> even more than our friends.

It's only in an age where faith is privatised outside of the community that a poem (?) like *Footprints* could be so popular. I know times in my life when Jesus has carried me, and it has meant more than I can say. But when I look back I see the footprints of the crowd of the community of the church carrying me.

There is nothing about this community that is voyeuristic. I am still mystified by the woman who left a service at St Laurence halfway through because, she told her friend, 'when I go to church I want to be anonymous'. Where on earth did she get that idea? Church is about participation. That's one of the reasons singing is so important.

While at theological college we had to attend chapel every morning, and to be honest it wasn't the early starts, but the downright boredom of the thing that kept me away. Anyhow, I remember that during one week when, apparently, attendance at chapel was particularly sparse, the Principal wrote to all of us say that when we withheld our presence from chapel we were robbing each other of the things God had for the community. I remember how we chortled at that over-dramatisation. It is only now, in church leadership, that I see the reality of that in people's non-participation. It's each other we are robbing. For here we have an essential contribution to make. If I don't give what God has given me to give, then we are less than we should and could be. This is the tragedy of gifts that God has given not being exercised; we are less when women aren't released to give what they can give, when gay people are alienated and when children are kept quiet.

Here, in community, my character is shaped and re-formed. And it's from this character that my action comes. The community creates the conditions for me to live out this life of following Jesus. In fact it's only possible here. All the ethical frameworks for the followers of Jesus – the stuff about money and power, about

humility and service, about giving and forgiving, about peaceful
reactions and patience, about trust and faithfulness, about holiness and goodness – they are only possible within the life of the
community. The New Testament never offers these ways of living
as personal plans for individual self-improvement. Any ethical
position is only made possible and made credible by the church.
Following Jesus is only possible with others.

Of course I concede that there are times when people need
time out, space to clear their heads, or leave one community to
throw their lot in with another. Church can only exist when it
nurtures a high-trust environment, allowing those such as a
wonderful eighteen-year-old known to St Laurence as Bobby
Love to say, 'Chris, I still support the team – I just haven't made it
to any home matches recently.'

The thing is, when we give up our ideals we are able to engage
with the reality. At St Laurence we sat round for a bit and
wondered when our heroes were going to arrive: when our
worship leader might be brought along, when the evangelist who
would bring in all the young people might pitch up, when the
true intercessors would turn up to kick-start the real stuff. We are
still waiting. Actually we've given up waiting. Because we realised
it's not about others, it's about us. That's the wonder of the gospel
– God uses people like us, in communities like these, to do his
will and push out the boundaries of his kingdom.

For a church is not an end in itself. We are primarily orientated around God and his life among us, and because of who this
God is we are turned inside out, living as his faithful witnesses in
the world. Too often church is just concerned with its own life: its
own health, its own relevance, its own troubles, its own demise.
The reformer Martin Luther defined an individual's sin as a heart
'curved in on itself'. In this regard the definition of a sinful
church is a church curved in on itself: preoccupied with its own
life, its own survival, its own self. A church lives on being
orientated around God and God's Kingdom.

Graham Cray once said, 'I don't care how high a view you
have of the church, as long as your view of the kingdom is
higher.' I think he means that the church serves the kingdom.

And that is what Jesus is about in his world. The church is the primary, but not the only, tool to see that come into being.

Again this is worked out in particular locations in particular ways. We ask ourselves the following question fairly regularly: what difference does it make to this town of Reading that we are located here? How is the presence of God in this community serving the kingdom of God in this area? Shane Claibourne, who deserves as wide a hearing as he can possibly get, issues a profound challenge when he says that if we lose a generation from the church it's not because they haven't been entertained, it's because they haven't been dared. Involvement in the kingdom is a dare of faith. But, as in Jesus, so in us; the Spirit comes to us for the sake of others.

The task of the church isn't to run outside the camp, gain converts and drag them to safety within the walls. Again, it's not anything so crude as being about numbers, or making sure we don't die out. It's about something so much bigger; God's kingdom.

But time and time again the church ducks the challenge and lives as some kind of gated community in the world. Listening to some 'theology' of the world this is hardly surprising; this world, we are told, is dark and evil. It is the realm of the Satan and leads people away from God. Really? Doesn't God love this world, doesn't he enjoy it and isn't he present here to us and for us? He loved it so much he counted it worthy of his own life, at the greatest personal cost. While there are things in this world that do give us cause to fear, to weep, to seek to bring transformation, safety and light, any idea of the church as God's safe house from the evil world must be resisted. You pointed out to me the other day a flier for a course for parents of teenagers called, 'How to drug-proof your teenager'. This is the church as a gated community, as a place where we batten down the hatches and barricade the doors for our own safety. And, as an aside, the people who run the course ought to be ashamed of themselves for playing on the fears of parents. Who can give guarantees like that?

But this is not the church that follows the pattern of Jesus Christ. This is not the community that lives and dares, that risks and strategises for the sake of the kingdom. This community sells everything for the pearl of great price, gives itself entirely for the field it's called to purchase, gambles everything on the King's reign. In my experience, this looks like teenagers being schooled in their own dignity, like teenage mothers knowing they won't have to raise their child on their own, like bucking the propaganda that you are of more value if you buy things of high value or get the right exam results, and like unmasking the lie that drink and drugs give you the best time. The church serves the kingdom, and the barricades the King still storms are in the places where indignity, worthlessness, despair and vicious circles boast their lying reign. As Claibourne says, 'the poor always have names'. Each church, each member of each church, needs to know the names of those they serve in the name of Christ. We don't just throw money, double click on 'contribute now' or pray generalities. We serve people with faces, whose names we hold in our hearts, whose cost we feel in our resources and whose weight we carry on our knees.

The gifts of each person in the church are harnessed by God for his kingdom. In fact that is what church exists for – to enable each person to make their difference. This is why I am always puzzled when we talk as if everyone's gift can be used simply to uphold, maintain and take forward the internal life of the church community. Churches would need to have less than forty members for that to be possible. No, church releases each of its members in the kingdom work that they have been called to do. For Mark that's in his teaching; he is called to push out the boundaries of the kingdom in enabling young people to take their place in the world as responsible adults. For Abs that's in her doctoring as she works to bring healing through oncology to those who respond well and to help children and families face the un-faceable in the last stages of life. For Michelle it's in mothering; enabling her to raise her three children as cherished, loved and believed-in young people. For you that's in … well, that's for you to work out within the community he calls you to. But each person's contribution to the furthering of the kingdom is vital. Rather than take up people's best time and resources, or give them the idea that what they do doesn't really count, the church stands behind them and alongside them to enable them to do what they're called to do with all of God's passion and skill.

The church, then is God's agent of transformation, for individuals and communities, for the environment and culture. The church is a champion of the oppressed and downtrodden, a justice-loving and righteousness-insisting collective which does not rest until all is made new. It's a place of healing where vicious circles get broken and the hopeless are reborn in vision. It's a dynamic of meaning and difference, a community of loving, self-giving, including, saving, merciful, forgiving and stretching people in a state of continual becoming.

The church exists to bear witness to Christ in the world. Sometimes we go about this in the wrong way. We get flattered by power and prestige, by so-called influence and find ourselves compromising for the sake of a prominent position in the church. You have always been rightly sceptical of those times the church seems aligned to closely with political power. For example, the capitulation of the German church to Nazism is certainly something to make us pause.

Of course there were those who stood against the church aligning themselves with Hitler, and they formed the confessing church in the 1930s – Barth, Bonhoeffer and Niemoller are the best known of these. But the fact they didn't all do it, the fact that only a minority stood against this compromise for power, this siding with the political leaders is enough to make us pause and remain silent for a couple of minutes. The church proclaims the good news of Christ, in every and all ways, always. We must not simply run errands for the world; we must not simply ingratiate ourselves so people like us.

If you have read this far, you have once again show your immense kindness to me. I am sorry if it has been a little too full on, or a little too personal. But it rises from my conviction that the church is God's principal means of transforming the local community. This is how he does it. Through people like you and me. The church is changing community, committed to seeing change one life at a time. My plea would not be simply that you, but that everyone that confesses the name of Jesus throws their lot in with a local community that bear their Lord's name. At the moment there are many who profess to follow Christ who seem to make a virtue of having as little to do with church as possible, of deconstructing church and refusing to take responsibility for the present and the future.

What the church will look like in the future is not known. But it won't look like this. A deconstructed church is a church embarrassed by itself. We must sit in respectful creativity with our past, and lightly enough with the present, that the generation to come can themselves take their place in shaping God's people. It's never about being relevant. It's always about being authentic. Authentic to God and to each other and to this kingdom.

Anthonia, I am sorry if it's embarrassing to be so specific. But it is specific. You won't know what you're looking for until you find yourself in his community. Taking your place among the people of God is what you were made for. And without you, we can't be what we were made for.

Don't spoil my girls too much,

Chris

4

Sin

To Jonny

Jonny is one of my oldest friends. He has most of the characteristics of Dr Gregory House, but with a few more relational skills. As well as being some kind of genius, he is loyal, kind and doesn't suffer fools for longer than two seconds. He is a brilliant journalist and thrives in a parallel universe of power players, breaking world events and headlines. He describes himself, rather triumphantly, as an atheist.

I have a sense that he is both fascinated and disturbed by my Christian faith; that one of his closest friends is a convinced follower of Jesus means that he can't dismiss Christianity quite as quickly as he might otherwise have brushed it aside. Often it will take over ten seconds for him to label me a 'loon'.

While the photographs were being taken at our wedding, I could tell something was bothering him. It didn't take long for me to get to the bottom of it; he had taken offence at the singing of 'Amazing Grace'. He was not, he insisted, out there on the lawn round the back of St John's Chichester, a 'wretch', and he did not need 'saving'. Neither was he 'lost' or 'blind'.

As lovely as he is, and as much as I value him being atheist/god-father to my second child, I beg to differ.

Dearest Jonny,

One of the hardest things for any of us is finding that our opinion of ourselves is different from the reality of what or who we really are.

I was in much too small a car, for much too long a journey, with way too many people, late one night coming back from Cardiff. We had gone to see a preacher called Rob Bell who had captured all of our hearts. Whether it was the imminent arrival of midnight, the toll five grown bodies were taking on a Nissan Micra or the fact we had travelled 120 miles there and 120 miles back for a 73-minute talk, by the time we hit the outskirts of God's own town of Reading we were all a bit irritable. We had a go at Nick, the driver, for his musical taste (there comes a time when you have heard enough obscure 'next big thing' music) Renie, for her navigational unskills and Westy for his flatulence, which had reached levels beyond measuring by any instruments in the scientific world. At the stretch of road alongside the big park, Westy came back with at me with, 'Well at least my halitosis breath doesn't singe my friends' eyelashes …'

Quiet descended like a mist. I hesitated. 'Are you saying I have bad breath …?'

There was silence from the other occupants of the car. Even Westy.

From nowhere one of my worst fears put its freezing hands into my body and gripped my heart. Did I have bad breath? Was I one of those people everyone tried not to stand too close to when I was talking to them? Did everyone try to breathe out, rather than in, around me? And, worst of all, *did everyone else know this about me except me*?

I couldn't wait to get out of the car. Once inside my house I lovingly shook Belinda awake and asked her about it. All she could say through her sleep was: 'I thought you knew'. Brilliant.

After brushing my teeth, my gums, my tongue and my lips for thirteen minutes I went to sleep, careful not to breathe too much on my pillow, unless I stained the linen with my foul breath, and aware that there was no going back from what I had found out that night about myself.

So, alongside my apology to you for my bad breath, comes to you my assurance, Jonny, that I know finding stuff out about yourself which you had either never entertained as true, or always hoped wouldn't be true, is a hard revelation to bear. That's never more true when coming to terms with the fact that we are sinners. I am, you are.

What I will try to do in these next pages is offer an explanation of why I think that is the case. I will do this firstly by arguing that 'sin' language is necessarily God language, and it presupposes certain truths about God's reality and involvement with his world. With such a backdrop, sin is recognised as a misplacing of God and a misaligning of our place, and his gifts, in his world. I will argue that, in the light of what we know about ourselves, the fact that we are sinners makes deep sense in describing our experience and prescribing our self-awareness. I will, however, set out that it is the life and death of Jesus that unveil our true, false condition, and reveal the need we have of a Saviour.

When Jesus is held up to our lives he acts as a plumb line, and what we gather about ourselves is a rather different perspective from the one we're inclined to give to ourselves. In this light, the darkness of sin is a terrible predicament which enslaves us and shames us, which breaches our relationship and in some kind of anti-Midas way, affects and pollutes everything we touch. However 'we celebrate not our sickness but our cure', so I will lay out the stronger stuff of forgiveness, redemption and resurrection.

You'll remember that in the centre of Reading, behind St Laurence's church, there is a public garden. On my way to the church building one day I wandered through the gardens and found myself in the midst of an eco-fair; all wormeries, recycled bottle tops and composters. At the far end I was drawn to this huge wooden wardrobe. Goodness knows how many people it had taken to carry there. And the car park was miles away. Anyhow, it turned out to be a confessional, with separate compartments for the confessor and confessant, curtain, grills, the works. Outside the box was a man with tie-dyed clothes and strange facial hair. I asked him what the idea was. He explained that 'dudes' were invited to go and sit in the confessional and confess how they had misused and exploited the environment. Then the conversation took an up for me and a down for him.

'Brilliant,' I said.

'Yeah man, we take it to all the festivals and you crazy cats love it. You go in and apologise for what you have done wrong to the planet. Then when you come out we agree a contract which you sign saying how you are going to change your behaviour towards the earth.'

'Brilliant,' I repeated, 'like repentance ...' The guy gives me a sideways look.

'Listen man, do you want to confess your sins or not?'

'Who am I confessing my sins to?'

'Well to me, or (motioning to his tie-dyed sister-in-arms) Sky.'

'But who am I really apologising to, saying sorry to? I mean, who have I wronged in mistreating the earth?'

'Uh ... I dunno, man.'

'What about God? The creator. The one who made everything. Maybe I should say sorry to God for mistreating his gift?'

'Listen it's just a gimmick. I mean ... oh, I've got to go and help out round the back.'

From our many conversations on this topic I know that the mention of God has you rubbing your hands, thinking you have won already. Because if the concept of sin is predicated on the existence of God, you can't even go 100 metres down this road with me; you're stopping right here. But, part of the joy of the letter is you can't interrupt, so at least get to the end and hear me out.

Sin is a God word. In our virtually secular culture it is not surprising that we do not talk of sin. We talk of weaknesses, slip-ups, indiscretions, flaws, shadow sides and mistakes. But to talk of 'sin' is to use a word that refers directly to God. In his stunning book *Bound to Sin*, Alistair McFadyen argues that our use, or otherwise, of the word 'sin' is a test of how we will let God define the world, for at heart when we talk of sin we are concerned with how we speak of God in this world.

> To ask whether the language of sin can have anything significant to say in addition to secular ways of speaking of the human condition which are pragmatically atheist, is to ask whether God, and talk of God makes any difference.

So Jonny, with your professed atheism, of course you'll struggle to grasp the concept of sin, because such a notion is built on the hypothesis that God is, and has clear intentions for and attention to the world. When the world we inhabit, and our being in it, is explained entirely without God, there is no need for this language. On top of living as if there were no God, there comes our dislike for language of blame and condemnation, our relativising of situations, our suspicion of authority that leads to the use of the word and concept of sin only in religious parodies.

The irony is that whatever language we use, we all know there is something wrong. We all feel deep down that things shouldn't be this way. And we feel it in those 'turn away from the screen now' moments when we are confronted with truly shocking details of humanity's lack of humanity in the ravages of war and revenge, in the 'can you believe it' tales of cruelty and shame, and the dull ache of helplessness we feel when word reaches us of some terrible disaster in which hundreds and hundreds of those with the same features as us are swept away. Surely on this we can agree; we are all too aware of the reality that things are not right. As Eugene Peterson writes in *Christ Plays in Ten Thousand Places:*

> It is impossible to find a single passage in history that displays humankind as sheer goodness, pure beauty, or flawless truth.

But I wonder whether the weight of what we know is too much to bear, so stumbling and blindfold, we grope about for some other explanation. And because we want to let ourselves off the hook, rather than naming wrong for what it is, we re-cast it. Instead of ruining life, it brings stimulation, interest and colour.

In so doing we fall for a huge illusion; that wrongdoing is more exciting than goodness. So we chuckle along with Ian Fleming who said in his introduction to a collection of essays on the deadly sins in the 1950s: 'How drab life would be without these sins, what dull dogs we all would be without a healthy trace of many of them in our makeup.' In his James Bond fantasy world, he might be able to keep this deceit going. Real life is

somehow different. For me the words of Simone Weil, the
twentieth-century French philosopher ring far truer:

> Imaginary evil is romantic and varied, real evil is
> gloomy, monstrous, barren and boring. Imaginary good
> is boring, real good is always new, marvellous,
> intoxicating.

There is not space here to sketch out in sufficient depth a
rationale for talking of the Satan and evil. It has been done in
other places, so much better by those more able (for example, by
N. T. Wright in *Evil and the Justice of God* and by C. S. Lewis in
The Screwtape Letters). But one of evil's most deadly triumphs is to
portray itself as more interesting than goodness. It is one of the
severest fallacies that goodness is inane, colourless and pedestrian.
I have always liked the line that argues there is actually nothing
original about sin, nothing creative or first hand about it. Rather,
it spirals into destruction and lifelessness in ever growing self-
obsession and slavery. But that evil is seen in the 'more than',
when wrongdoing creates a momentum which picks up pace
until it's out of control. How often have we heard confessions that
one thing led to another – things weren't supposed to have got so
out of hand, but people felt powerless to stop it?

Sin, wrongdoing, evil is not just the lack or absence of
goodness, nor is it simply projection. Its wounds and scars are too
deep for us to be able to accept that. In one hundred bloody days
in Rwanda in 1994 800,000 Tutsis were murdered; I buried a
fifteen-year-old girl who had been shot in the park; thousands
were killed in the siege of Sarajevo and Srebrenica; I took a
funeral for a seventeen-year-old who was stabbed to death in
Reading town centre; millions were extinguished by Hitler,
Stalin, Pol Pot, Mau and Amin because of their race or religion;
our friend was forced into a car by a man she didn't know, driven
to a lonely area and raped. This is not an absence of something we
are talking about. This is a destructive, craved, violent, selfish,
tyrannical, abusive, and debilitating curse, and its poison courses
through the veins of our world's history and present life.

What's more, we are aware that it's not just out there that things aren't the way they should be, but inside our very selves; the poison courses through our own veins. While publicly we try to put clear water between ourselves and those who commit horrendous deeds, while we use broad black brushstrokes to portray them as 'evil', 'inhuman' and 'monsters', we dare not admit that it is our shared humanity that scares us so much about what they have done. It's our propensity to do the same that most offends us. Humanity's major problems do not arise simply from powerlessness, ignorance, the unfair distribution of wealth or the lack of human rights, but from our very own selfish hearts. Whilst, along with the Mumfords, we are all scared of what we will discover inside, facing the dark truth of ourselves in the point the light breaks in.

With this refusal to fudge the issue, to let ourselves off the hook, we can do something we desperately need to do; to face ourselves and our world and feel the gap between how things are and how we sense they should be. All those who have been part of unimaginable events of torture, genocide, cruelty and abuse testify to the need to confront what is wrong. There must be no brushing under the carpet, no excuses or papering over the cracks. This is not simply to address the seriousness of what takes place. It is to give sufficient weight to what causes it, and what it can lead to.

Sin is what is done against God and God's ways. It is not so much a description of individual actions or behaviours, as a state of our own making. We sin because we are sinners. It's not an accusation or a condemnation. Rather it's a diagnosis; a revelatory insight into our condition. And our decision to take this route is explained in the third chapter of Genesis.

Now, I know that by this point you will have had numerous problems with what I've said (which, as I've said, is the joy for me of writing a letter that you can't interrupt!) Introducing ancient texts of scripture to back up my case will take the game to love-forty in your favour, with you serving. And you will think you can serve me an ace because you automatically assume my argument is going to be built on taking some story of a snake standing up and talking as literal fact. But to do that to one of the most powerful stories in the world, which has shaped our understanding of who we are and why we do what we do, is to completely misunderstand it. When we are in the realms of these opening chapters of the Jewish and Christian Bible, we are in some of the wisest, deepest, most profound waters literature has ever known. It is not about their historicity. It is about the truth that they tell. And millions and millions of us would contend that they tell us the truth about what we are.

The wonderful creation poems of Genesis 1–2 have painted our genesis in the most vivid colours and the broadest brush-strokes. This world is God's good handiwork, called into being from nothing, in deliberate and definite love by God. There is the dynamic of blessing. Everything is good. All is well. God, humanity and the creation exist in real relationship. Evil is not part of this picture. The inference is that what we now experience as the feeling that things should not be this way is not part of the original design. That things have gone wrong is not caused by a design fault, a hairline fracture within the creation or a manufacturer's error which has missed its recall.

For humanity has an ability to choose either for the things of God or against them. This freedom is a vital part of God's loving of those he made in his image. It is real and exists in complimentarity with God's freedom. The two do not compromise one another, although it's generally assumed that God's freedom to be God and our freedom to be human are not able to co-exist. We fall for the trick that we can only be free when we have taken God's position and put ourselves in his place.

Enticed by the temptation that they can 'be like God' (Genesis 3:5) the woman and man eat the fruit of the tree they have been forbidden to eat. They become aware of their nakedness and shame; they hide, and when found, refuse to take responsibility for what they have done, each passing the blame quickly. The consequences of what they have done are spelt out in terms that affect their relationship with God, with each other and with the non-human creation. 'Sin is the de-relational act *par excellence*', says Eugene Peterson in *Christ Plays in Ten Thousand Places*.

Instead of living under blessing, there is a cycle of curse hanging over all they do, leading to death.

This resonates entirely with the reality of what I observe and take part in. The sense that our selfishness isn't a natural part of us is echoed in our sense that our hearts are made for better than to be curved in on themselves. That there is something baffling in our choosing to go against God and his ways. Why we would choose against One that bought us into being and whose intentions for us are nothing but good? But we do. Here we are able to be silent at the mystery of why we choose to do such evil deeds. There is something inexplicable in much human sinfulness, and we can try to explain away it too quickly and too easily, even with the wisest psychology or the most profound understanding of social conditions. That we can turn away from the life that is offered to us in God is, as Karl Barth said, the 'impossible possibility'.

What entices us is the false promise that we can be gods. I am persuaded by McFadyen's thesis that sin is basically misplaced praise. We refuse to orientate ourselves around God; rather we orientate ourselves around ourselves and our desires. We place the good gifts of God in the centre of our world and make our choices around them. These gifts, in themselves good, were never meant to bear the weight of being the centre for our world, and when good things are worshipped as if they were God, they become idols. If you want to see where someone's idols are look for what people sacrifice to – for idols always demand sacrifice. But they never deliver what they promise. So we see the havoc wreaked upon lives and cultures by the worship of wealth and possessions, of looking young and beautiful, of sex and pleasure, of power and influence.

Sin is always oversold; there is deceit at the core of it. The lie is that we can live in the true God's world as mini-gods, under our own authority, making our own rules, declaring ourselves as right and others as wrong, sitting in judgement over others and placing ourselves and our own desires very much at the centre of the world. It is a temptation we all succumb to, insist upon, defend and glory in. We can use the gifts of God without reference to God, for our own sake. When confronted with our actions we feel shame, and so quickly blame anyone else but ourselves, establishing highly sophisticated systems of defence and refusing to take responsibility. The consequences of all this on our place in God's world, our misuse of creation, our relationships with one another and our relating to the true God are too horrific to truly be contemplated. It hardly needs saying that sin affects all of our pasts, presents and futures.

It is not in the abstract that we contemplate the consequences of sin. It is not even as it is writ large in the history books, newspaper headlines and breaking news that scrolls along the bottom of the TV, but in the life and death of Jesus of Nazareth. Obviously we're now revisiting the person who you and I have spent more time talking about than any other (other than perhaps our children). But I can't apologise for that, for Jesus of Nazareth is the plumb-line for our humanity.

Here is one who shows us that being selfish and egotistical, corrupt and deceitful is not part of our essential humanity. While we use the excuse 'I'm only human' for our daily shortcomings, Jesus' life shows us that's not a good enough excuse. No, this one is fully human, yet sin has no hold on him. Yet he is like us, one of us, our brother, one made of the same fickle stuff as we are. He uses his freedom not to do anything he wants to do, but to do the right thing, thus stomping on our ludicrous idea that freedom means being able to make any choice you want to. He uses his freedom to enter our place of slavery.

One of my favourite pictures of Johnny Cash is of him being baptized in the Jordan. It was probably the fourth time he had been baptized, which by most peoples reckoning is around three times too many, but such was the pull of the Jordan. Jesus' baptism in this river marks the beginning of his public ministry in all four Gospels. That he chooses to be baptized is baffling unless he is using his freedom to enter our prison.

Baptism was a ritual that John made his own. There are different ideas tracing where he might have got the practice from, but what is clear is that if you were baptized by John, you were getting yourself ready for the return of YHWH to his people. And this particular form of getting ready was repentance, an about turn, a public confession of the individual's intention to mend their ways. So when a thirty-something man came to join the queue for baptism, everyone assumed that he was just another sinner coming for repentance.

Yet Jesus had done nothing wrong to turn from. It makes sense only if he did it not for his own sin, but to be counted amongst the sinners. Jesus didn't explain what he was doing. He was happy to be labelled a sinner. Here, he took upon himself the sins of the world. It was this act of baptism, of taking on sinful humanity, that would eventually see him on a cross. This is why the days after the baptism tell of a full-scale assault by the Satan on Jesus, seeking to tempt and entice him to go a different way. The Satan knew all would be lost if this one went through death. But Jesus freely entered our condition, for it is not outside of us that the healing needs to take place, but within. I said earlier that we can concoct the most elaborate arguments to deny responsibility. Yet here is one who freely chose to take responsibility for things he had never done.

My challenge to you then, is not to consider sin in the abstract, as some philosophical or theological term, nor even in the practicalities of what we see, and you report, day by day, but in the life and death of the man Jesus. Doing so makes for ugly viewing, but ultimately there is nothing more beautiful than what we see.

For at heart there is a realisation that sin and evil cannot be solved or healed, redeemed or repaired by developmental progress of evolution, as if the world were on some upward projection, getting increasingly better, evolving ourselves towards some Utopia. If anything we have more to despair about. Sin spirals into a tighter curve into itself; the circles seem to get more vicious and we sense ourselves more impotent to see them broken. And then God comes among us to do what we could not do; to redeem, to heal, to remake and break the cycles.

But it is not pretty; for here we are unmasked. Here the desperate, ugly, devastating consequences of our selfishness are writ large, nailed up in front of everyone. Jesus, the innocent one, the loving one, the kind and generous one, the hospitable one, the tenacious one, the courageous one, the wise one, the authentic one, is turned on by those around him. A close friend betrays, a best friend denies, witnesses lie, soldiers torture, crowds bay for blood, passersby mock, rulers save their jobs. Everyone tries to save themselves except Jesus, who seems eerily in control of all that is being done to him. This is what we do to goodness incarnate among us, this is what we do to honesty and right living – we crucify it. This is what sin is, what it does, what it means and how it gets its way. With all these people seeing their own selves as their own priority, establishing themselves as the most important person in the world, these god-pretenders try to force the true God out of the world.

At its heart sin is this banishing of God from his world. For he will not simply accept the non-speaking walk-on part we might be happy with him playing. This is his world and we are his people. God made us to live with God as our God, one we know and love, relate to and follow. Our choice against that is not inane or merely unfortunate; it is diabolical. It results in the severest of all breaches of life; a broken relationship with the God who made us, which necessarily cuts us off from life, from each other and from our future. In a word, death.

On the cross of Jesus Christ we see what sin does. We see that the choice to live our own way, to satisfy ourselves first, to save ourselves, to prioritise our needs, desires and reputation, is to involve ourselves in activities that lead to destruction. Sins are those actions that have no future, that have nothing redeeming latent within them. Lust is sexual desire without committed relationship; lies have no future in the light of the truth, gossip turns back to bite the gossiper, violence spirals into further violence, amassing wealth creates an insatiable thirst for more. The choice made against living God's way and choosing to live our own devastates families and communities, nations and corporations, friendships and the environment. And it devastates God. It is ugly because I am confronted with myself, with what I do and with the consequences. Jesus is not killed by the scum of humanity, but by people like me. In fact, I cause this death. As much as I might try to wash them, my hands are covered with blood.

For here, this innocent one becomes broken. With the theme of Genesis 3 ringing in the thunder, once again around a tree this representative of humanity makes a choice, but this time for right and good; he takes the responsibility and the blame. And so he becomes a lighting conductor, not for the vengeful wrath of God, but for the horrendous dehumanising torment of evil. Here the brokenness of the world is absorbed, the poison in the sea is drunk, the cutting down of God's good creation and making out of it an instrument of torture is enacted, the vicious circle reaches its essential outcome; abandonment, forsakenness, separation and death. God bears the consequences for something he never did.

And as he dies everything changes. And I mean everything. And I mean really changes.

The murmurs of change are music to our ears; they turn our head and increase the pulse of our heart. But the actuality of change and the delivery of it defies presidents and political programmes, plans and schemes. So I want to be clear to you about the change we are talking of. And to do this I need to introduce two words which might make you put this letter down, so if you need to, go and get yourself a strong drink now.

Good. Welcome back.

In the red corner we have *noetic*, in the blue corner we have *ontic*. Let me introduce them.

> *Noetic* refers to what goes on in our minds, our understanding, how we think about things.
> *Ontic* refers to how something is in its very self, in its being.

So *noetic* change is change which occurs in our comprehending, in our thinking and understanding. We gain new perspective and new ways of mentally approaching something. *Ontic* change is change in the very fibre of the substance of being. It is a shift or transformation not just in how something is viewed, but in the very thing itself.

In the death and resurrection of Jesus both these changes occur. And, once again, rather than try to sketch this out in the abstract, they find their traction in the real life of the world. So let us consider the painful reunion of the denier and the denied.

John tells how after the crucifixion of Jesus and the rumours of resurrection three days later, Jesus' followers were at a loose end. They decided to return to their home villages, and to their old professions. So they got out the nets and boats and set out for a fishing trip on Lake Galilee. They caught nothing. Again. A stranger on the shore urged them to throw their nets over the other side of the boat. They did so and caught more fish than they could hold (153 – that's why your school had 153 scholars). They recognised Jesus as the one who gave the angling advice and got to the shore as quickly as they could. There Jesus cooked breakfast for them and round the fire on which it was cooked they ate. John doesn't record a lot of dialogue. It seems the event was as charged as much with what wasn't being said as what was. Then came this conversation with Peter, the thrice denier.

> When they had finished eating, Jesus said to Simon Peter, 'Simon son of John, do you truly love me more than these?'
>
> 'Yes, Lord,' he said, 'you know that I love you.' Jesus said, 'Feed my lambs.'
>
> Again Jesus said, 'Simon son of John, do you truly love me?' He answered, 'Yes, Lord, you know that I love you.' Jesus said, 'Take care of my sheep.'
>
> The third time he said to him, 'Simon son of John, do you love me?' Peter was hurt because Jesus asked him the third time, 'Do you love me?' He said, 'Lord, you know all things; you know that I love you.'
>
> Jesus said, 'Feed my sheep. I tell you the truth, when you were younger you dressed yourself and went where

you wanted; but when you are old you will stretch out
your hands, and someone else will dress you and lead
you where you do not want to go.' Jesus said this to
indicate the kind of death by which Peter would glorify
God. Then he said to him, 'Follow me!'

(John 21:15–19)

Peter was the mouthy one, the confident one, the one who
boasted, just a couple of hours before he publicly claimed never
to have met Jesus, that he undoubtedly loved Jesus more than any
of his other friends, and that even if everyone else ran away he
would never do so (Mark 14:29ff.). And he wasn't trying to lie.
He surely believed it. For this rock of a man, the arrest of Jesus,
his trial and torture and his death, and Peter's part in the events
showed him quite a different picture of himself. It was the
harshest of mirrors held up to his face; he was the person he
didn't want to be. As Martin Luther says, 'the cross tests everything', particularly ourselves. The quest for truth can be frighten-
ing, and it must not be confused with sincerity, as Father de Luba,
an early Christian mystic said: 'It is not sincerity but truth which
frees us.'

On top of this noetic change, the new information Peter had
about himself was the deep wound which came from him having
let his master and friend down. He had thought that Jesus' death
had cut off any possibility of these things ever being addressed and
forgiven. How much of Peter died with Jesus?

Since that bad Friday, the rumours and visitations of a resurrected Jesus had provided a glimmer of hope that things might be
resolved. But there was also the fear of having to face one who
knew the truth of who he was. So Peter went back to the sea, to
the nets, to the boats; to the old day and night job. In this story he
was back where he was at the beginning, pre-Jesus. And it's
almost as if none of it had ever happened.

We haven't got time to concern ourselves with the first part of
the story, simply to point out that they were back at the beginning of the cycle; night, no fish, no catch, no hope. The empty
nets, the deep darkness of night, the desolation of not knowing

how things could ever change. They were back where they started, but it was even more painful, given all they had learnt. But into this cycle came the risen Jesus. Peter, who when he first met Jesus some three years before had asked him to go away from him because he was sinful, could have had little comprehension of how sinful he would be revealed to be. But the sight of Jesus now made him dive into the water. He wanted this sorted out and he knew he was safe with Jesus. This is, I think, part of the liberation that God's grace brings us; we are free to accept what is most unacceptable about ourselves. For in his company we are welcomed.

As W. H. Auden allegedly said:

> I love to sin; God loves to forgive.
> The world is admirably arranged.

Part of our difficulty in taking responsibility for the things we have done, is our shame – that *we* are the kind of people who do *these* kind of things. So many people are locked away in the prison of their own shame, which David Ford and Daniel Hardy described in *Living in Praise* as the 'implosion of respect', but with this crucified and risen one we are free not to hide our shame, but to come clean. I can breathe a sigh of relief that I can stop pretending that I am a better man than I truly know myself to be. I have been found out, but by one who is welcoming to me. Rather than my shame precluding me from God, it is my entry point. Stronger than my despair at what I find out about myself is the light in which I am bathed in by the one who knows what I am truly like yet loves me to death and beyond.

But Peter needed more than just breakfast. He needed to have what he had done addressed. So Jesus took him aside. The setting for Peter's biggest failure was around the fire in the High Priest's courtyard; here they were once more around a fire. Peter denied he knew Jesus three times; in this passage he is asked the same question three times. Peter was so called by Jesus as Peter means Rock; that name was dropped, for the previous Simon. The question was excruciating; 'Do you love me more than these?'; it's exactly what he had claimed those days before. But had he learnt? Had he faced himself?

The only thing Simon Peter could appeal to was Jesus' knowledge of him. 'Lord you know ...' And so we see forgiveness at work. A forgiveness which doesn't sweep the wrong under the carpet, which refuses not to mention it, or pretend it doesn't matter. No wrongdoing matters. Sin costs. It must be faced.

But here comes the ontic change. We are not simply given information about ourselves, we are remade. For the truth of Simon Peter had been revealed, and was truly faced. He was accepted and received in this state, not by someone who had been a third party to what has gone on, to what he has done, but by someone who was who was on the receiving end of the consequences of his sin. Things have changed because this one has somehow borne the cost of our choices, our failings and our shame. This one forgives and bears and absorbs because he himself carried the consequences of what has been done. He embodies the forgiveness he offers in himself. It is his to give, for he has won it.

And so in the death and resurrection of this Jesus, Simon Peter was remade. The dawn broke on a different day. The vicious circle was broken. An end has been made to sin with his death, evil has done its monstrous worst, to hell with evil and death and sin. And the one to whom our sinful rebellion is directed holds out his hands which bear the scars which speak of the cost of forgiveness, and loves us, and welcomes us, and remakes us and redeems us.

So here's the thing, Jonny. Although I have banged on about it in this letter, sin is not the most important thing that can or must be said about us. Neither is our failure, our shame, the possibility and actuality of our corrupt hearts; for through the cross and resurrection of Jesus even the sin of humanity crucifying God is creatively reworked by God into the event in which the very power of sin and death are themselves overcome. Here the blind are given sight, the lost are found, that which we cannot do for ourselves is secured by the gift of God.

Our present and our futures are not destined to be defined by our past mistakes. A new way forward is opened up and held out to us. Who we are and what we do, as individuals, communities and the world, is not determined by the darkness in our lives, but by the thousand fresh starts we are given, freely and graciously in the one whose love and forgiveness are stronger than death. In God's dealings with us sin is not diminished, but it is no longer definitive; it is rather salvation that is definitive.

It is this actuality, this new state of affairs totally beyond our power to bring about, which led an ex-slave trader called John Newton, to write the words I dream we'll one day join our voices to sing as you stand beside me:

> Amazing grace! How sweet the sound,
> That saved a wretch like me!
> I once was lost but now am found
> Was blind, but now I see.

With great love,

Chris

5

Seamless

To Nick

I met Nick at a big whoopty-do Christian festival. He is lovely. He's a bit of a golden boy. He is also a bit of a conference king, a bit of a Mr Toad – his eyes are always scanning the horizon for the next big thing. And it's always somewhere else.

Once he opened a talk by lamenting how mundane and pedestrian his life was and how guilty he felt about the gap between his reality and the exciting, highly-charged life he should be leading. He talked about how, if he was really 'spiritually on fire', he would rise above the mundanity of his day-to-day life, to the stuff that really counted for something. He would be seeing 'breakthrough' on a regular basis; he would be able to stop and heal the person who hobbled past him, to convert the man who ran the newsagent and prophesy over those stickily crushed against him in the tube. To illustrate what his life should be like, he went on to regale us with story after story of impressive and inspiring things that were happening in other places in the world. But I have to confess I wasn't really listening.

I was just transfixed by the weight of believing that the life that you were called to live was completely other and different than the one you were living.

Dear Nick,

I am sorry that last time we talked I didn't have time to hear all about your latest trip. From the brief conversation we had, the things that are happening in that place you visited in the States sound quite phenomenal, and it's clear it has had a deep impact on you. However, I have been musing on it for some time and wondered if you wouldn't mind if I tugged on the end of a couple of loose threads that were left hanging after our last conversation.

While there are many wonderful and inspiring things we can and need to learn from other places and perspectives, I guess if I am really honest, I have been increasingly concerned with your preoccupation with everywhere else except the place you're in. It sounds as if you're dissatisfied with your day-to-day life, and you've fallen for the idea that if you were really in God's 'zone' things would be radically different. Much more spiritual. And that in God's zone things are big and dramatic and decisive.

Instead I want to suggest that the Christian life is about living an integrated life, and that Jesus is the model for that. I have a real beef with the idea that God is simply interested in igniting a so-called 'spiritual' bit of us. By my reckoning, if we are talking about spiritual things, we are not talking about one part of us, but all of us. I am convinced that the Christian life is not about hankering to be somewhere different, but about us taking seriously where we are. And prayer is the place where we get rooted. In it all I am going to assume that what you most long for is integration with what God wants from you and your present life now.

So let me start by pulling this thread. Last time I saw you, you were wearing a rather fine shirt. So do me a favour – that shirt you are wearing now, just check the label. Not the Hollister logo, but the wash label, and then check what it's made of, and where it's made.

I've just checked my shirt; for the record mine is 64 per cent cotton, 31 per cent polyamide, 3 per cent elastane and 2 per cent metallic fibres. I have also just learnt it was made in Bangladesh. To differing extents, all of the above disquiets me (but obviously not enough for me to stop wearing the shirt). Put to the side the question of taste – this one usually gets the thumbs down from the girls. (Last week as I came downstairs ready for an evening out, I got a, 'Dad. Seriously?' from my six-year-old daughter.) But how about the biblical opposition to my shirt?

'Keep my decrees … Do not wear clothing woven of
two kinds of material.'

(*Leviticus 19:19*)

I think I gave you a copy of the wonderfully entertaining book by
A. J. Jacobs, *TheYear of Living Biblically: One Man's Humble Quest to
Follow the Bible as Literally as Possible*. In Jacobs' quest to live by the
rules of the Bible for a year, one of the first things he does is to
invite a Mr Berowitz round to his NewYork apartment to give his
present wardrobe the once-over in the light of this command.
Mr Berowitz is a *shatnez* tester – he checks for mixed fabrics.
Many of Jacobs' garments have to be put away for the year
because they break this commandment. When Jacobs asks
Mr Berowitz why this command is in the Jewish scriptures he
replies, 'I have no idea.'

Neatly sidestepping the onerous matter of the application of
OldTestament law to today, I wonder if I might suggest a reason?
The thing behind the thing, as Rob Bell would say. Is this
requirement for unadulterated garments that are true and genu-
ine, made out of the same stuff through and through, unified to
the last fibre, an expression of desire on God's behalf for consist-
ency?

We don't know what Jesus wore. Although my guess is that it
wasn't white, and if my shirt had been available and in the right
fabrics, he would have given it a go. After all, he didn't have
daughters to battle with. But we do know that in those days, men
would have worn a linen undergarment which they would have
washed regularly and over that they would have worn some kind
of tunic. All we know of what Jesus wore comes from an aside, as
John tells of his last moments;

> When the soldiers crucified Jesus, they took his clothes,
> dividing them into four shares, one for each of them,
> with the undergarment remaining. This garment was
> seamless, woven in one piece from top to bottom.

> 'Let's not tear it,' they said to one another. 'Let's decide
> by lot who will get it.'

This happened that the scripture might be fulfilled which said,

'They divided my clothes among them
and cast lots for my garment.'
So this is what the soldiers did.

(John 19:23–24)

Jesus had a seamless undergarment. Some suggest that a Jewish mother would make her son a garment when he left home for the first time, others that the seamless robe was a traditional piece of clothing worn by Galilean men. We do know that most garments for men were made from two pieces of cloth, as first-century looms could not make a piece of cloth big enough to cover a grown man. A seamless robe was made from two pieces of cloth where the seams had been integrated and woven together so as to disappear. It took more time, and so the garment was more pricy.

As well as some inside information about Jesus, might this not also be some insight into how he lived? Does this seamless robe not stand for Jesus' seamless life, showing that he lived a harmonious life, without joins and separation?

On the face of it there is something desperate about the only thing Jesus had left being taken from him. On the other, is it not significant that, in his hour of death, the soldiers did not tear up what he had worn daily? Such was his integrity and strength. He had lived in a seamless way, without contradiction, without division, and called others to do the same.

Nick, you live in London. London is a cacophony of places side by side: council estates next door to gated communities, affluent shopping streets dissected by roads with market stalls, enclaves of different communities living in delineated space side by side. This isn't just true of where we live. It's true of our way of living. We live our lives by separating out, by dividing, by compartmentalising.

I remember reading an article in the *Guardian* recalling a conversation President Bill Clinton had while travelling on Air Force One to the opening of the Atlanta Olympics. During the plane journey, he was asked by a member of the press which Olympic event he would choose to compete in. Without hesitation he said, 'The Decathlon, because you had there ten different disciplines that you could concentrate on.' The observation was made that Clinton is the embodiment of the modern-day lifestyle choice called compartmentalisation: he is peace-maker and missile-launcher, friend of Israel and trusted confidant of the Palestinians. He is at the same time a social conservative and liberal, adulterer, good father, loyal husband, lousy husband. The liar, the truth-teller, the former leader of the free world, the imprisoned man who seems incapable of not acting out his passions.

But while we might see it in Bill Clinton with harsh clarity, our culture abounds within compartments. Madonna claimed to be 'at least' ten different people. When I threw this in, as a natty aside, during a conversation with a public representative, he remarked, 'She is lucky she only has to be ten people. I have to be at least twenty.' There are as many different areas of our lives as there are sections of a Sunday newspaper; professional and private, social and internal, family and company, past and present, leisure and luxury. We can live as totally different people depending on who we are with and what is required of us.

Despite this, throughout western culture there is a deep hunger to live authentically: to live an integrated life, to live in rhythm, to live 'truly'.

But we say this as if we know what that 'truly' means.

Our society considers that the most important ethical question for individual consideration is that most instinctual of questions; 'How can I be true to myself?' This is the fatal flaw of confusing being real for being true. In the midst of this longing for integration, there are so many things which disconnect us from ourselves, our fellow human beings, and God. Indeed, in *Making All Things New* (I think I might have lent it to you once) Henri Nouwen declared, 'our paralyzing sense of separation constitutes the core of much human suffering.'

I think this is what you are seeking in your constant attention to where the truly spiritual life is being lived. But my sense is that the common take on faith doesn't heal this, but compounds this. Rather than bringing the desired coherence and harmony, faith has often done the opposite. The Christian faith is seen as simply one compartment, the 'God-y' bit of us – the religious supplement, the 'spiritual' bit. And what the truly 'spiritual' do is feed the God compartment so much that nothing else matters. The other day I heard a national Christian speaker say he was 'bi-locational' – the 'fleshly' bit of him lived on the earth, while his spiritual side resided in heaven. And the worst thing was, everyone nodded as if he was right.

A few miles from where you live in the London is the wonderful National Gallery. There are some immensely historic works of art. Eighty per cent of them have religious subjects. If you listen to old-school classical music, by far the majority was composed for religious use. Four hundred years ago the best that human gifts produced, whether in architecture, art or music, were orientated around God. Because God answered the questions of existence, of creation, of meaning, of explanation. But when Immanuel Kant, an eighteenth-century German philosopher with a rather huge forehead, summed up things for the enlightened generation by clarifying that the only things we could be really sure of were things we could prove, God was excluded, as he lay outside the realms of such empirical research. This didn't mean that Kant that didn't believe in God's existence, it just meant that he didn't see God as part of the day-to-day stuff of life. God's realm was behaviour and ethics. So God was relegated, pushed out little by little.

As science, modern medicine and the like started to find the answers to the things that God had been the explanation for – creation and human nature for example – the space God was given to occupy became less and less. This is what the modern-day saint Dietrich Bonhoeffer calls, the 'God of the gaps' theory; historically God was used to explain the gaps in our understanding, but as other rational and scientific explanations came up to explain the gaps, the need or space for God became less and less, particularly in the public arena. Added to this the penchant humanity has always had for dualism – for dividing reality into the sacred and the secular, the religious pursuits and the worldly, the spiritual and the profane – and we have a cocktail which leaves God out in the cold, and the things he concerns himself with out of this world. Bonhoeffer wrote from Tegel prison in 1944:

> I'm often reluctant to mention God by name to religious people – because that name somehow seems to me here not to ring true, and I feel myself to be slightly dishonest (it's particularly bad when others start to talk in religious jargon; I then dry up almost completely and feel awkward and uncomfortable) – to people with no religion I can on occasion mention him by name quite calmly and as a matter of course. Religious people speak of God when human knowledge has come to an end, or when human resources fail – in fact it is always the *deus ex machina* that they bring on the scene, either of the apparent solution of insoluble problems, or as strength in human failure … It seems to me that we are trying anxiously in this way to reserve some space for God …'

Reserving some place for God has been baptised by talk of humans having a 'God-shaped hole'. It leads me to make Pascal, to whom it is attributed, prominent in my book of villains. The concept has become a beloved illustration used in evangelism; we are all born with a God-shaped hole, the deepest part of us that yearns for God, and we try to fill it with many other things – wealth, relationships, career, aspirations, and of course sex and pleasure – but none of those can fill it adequately. There will always be this underlying hunger, for only God can fill the God-hole. In other schemes of life this God-shaped hole was called the soul, the 'spiritual' bit of us.

Unwittingly what all this has done is to reduce God's place to a part of life, a religious section. So God becomes an addition, about something more than what we have.

Sometimes, we in the church have encouraged such a take on faith, by suggesting that questions of God are most profoundly stimulated when we look outside of normal life, because there must be something more than this. Of course there is more than this.

But it's not out there.

About that.

But in here.

About this.

In the scheme of things, where God concerns himself with the 'more than this', God concerns himself primarily with the so-called spiritual things. Of course they affect the physical, the day-to-day, but primarily they are located out of sight, and out of the public realm. God concerns himself with our interior life, our private life, our personal life; our spirituality.

You recommended that my wife attend a conference run by people who had the confidence to call what they were doing 'Jesus Ministry International'. One could be forgiven, from reading the handouts, in assuming that Jesus simply came to bring a superior system of healthcare and a cleaned-up and stimulating internal life. There is no mention in nine pages of justice, money, non-violence, poverty, and how we might treat other people. How dare they?

My problem with all of this is that it reduces God's stuff to an optional extra part of life. A bolt on. The God App. My friend Marie once turned away people from a local church who knocked on her door to tell her about Jesus with the simple truism that she didn't have time or space in her life for anything else at the moment. Life was so full with how she raised the kids, how she made a living, family relationships, moving house and work that there wasn't any space for anything else. They said they would come back in a couple of years when things had calmed down.

But God is not about something else. He is about my 'this'. I find his place within life not with an existential sigh, 'there must be more than this'. But by weighing how he actually interacts with my 'this'.

You see, Nick, as long as we consider the things that God truly wants for us and from us to be beyond what life is now, we will not see the here and now as the primary place of his location and his work. God and his dealings seem to be a million miles away from the push and pull of real life; they are in some other realm. So I sling Bonhoeffer your way again:

> It seems to me that we are trying anxiously in this way to reserve some space for God ... I should like to speak of God not on the boundaries but at the centre, not in weakness but in strength, and therefore not in death and guilt but in man's life and goodness.

I spent dreamy days as an undergraduate in the Theology department at the University of Durham, literally a snowball's throw away from the cathedral, which is generally regarded as this nation's favourite building. During a seminar I was leading, my professor turned his chair towards me, set me in his sights and said:

'Christopher, I am puzzled to discern what you think God concerns himself with in the world. Where is God to be found?'

Without hesitation I gave him the correct answer: 'God lives in the hearts of believers and in the church.'

'Anywhere else?' he asked me (I took the raised eyebrows as a sign I was on the right lines).

'No.'

He suggested I went away and read a book called the Bible and came back the next week with a more Christian answer.

The realm of God is not reduced simply to our internal life. Or the people that bear his name. The stuff that God concerns himself with is the stuff of this life. Scripture attests to this again and again. God's people live in specific situations, and his work works itself out in particular places: Eden, Ur, Bethel, Bethlehem, Egypt, Jericho, Nineveh, Jerusalem, Galilee, Antioch, Athens and Rome, to name but a few. God's ways and means are not about somewhere else, they are about here. They are not about a 'more than', they are about what is at hand. He is not a God of the gaps, he's a God of the centre. It's not about a God-shaped hole, it's about God-shaped lives. Jesus doesn't talk about internal spirituality – he talks about the Kingdom of God.

As Bonhoeffer explains, Christianity is profoundly 'this worldy' because of Jesus. The problem with the God of the gaps theology is that 'It conceded to the world the right to determine Christ's place within the world.' (Bonhoeffer again.) That's the wrong way round. Instead it is Christ who determines God's place in this world.

Here is one who lives seamlessly a fully God-shaped life, and he does so in the middle of this world. He is surrounded by people who are aggravating and frustrating, in situations that are less than ideal and downright unfair. God does this enfleshed. In a body. When God desires to show us himself and his ways, he does not bring some enlightenment by which men and women can leave the profanity of this world; he does not impart some spiritual exercises by which we can be free of the trappings of this life: rather 'The word became flesh and made his dwelling among us' (John 1:14). In *The Message* Eugene Peterson tries to get the sense of the Old Testament idea of the tabernacle by saying 'The word became flesh and blood, and moved into the neighbour-hood.'

The incarnation has always caused trouble for people. For some, it cannot be imagined that Jesus was truly God conceived, so utterly opposed to God is the physicality of the bodies we inhabit. No, such an argument goes, the spiritual is the pure stuff. To be holy is to rise out of the chaos and burdens on our bodies, to be free from the here and now. The trouble is that this thinking owes far more to Plato than Jesus Christ. In Jesus, God stands before us not wearing a mask, not veiled, but face to face. To look at Christ's face is to look into the face of God.

A bishop called Arian put his name to the heresy that Jesus couldn't have been fully God. Another camp said Jesus couldn't have been fully human. Both beliefs come from the idea that this world and God do not, cannot, will not, must not, mix. But Jesus, this body-inhabiting God, stands in front of us as fully human, going through all we go through, struggling with all we struggle with (and the rest), and proclaims: matter matters. This is shown in his birth, his life, his death and his resurrection. In *Following Jesus* Tom Wright says: 'It's terrorists and tyrants who blow the world up. It's God who puts it back together.'

In fact, in his book *Ethics*, Bonhoeffer goes so far as to say this:

> the reality of Jesus Christ comprises the reality of the world within itself. The world has no reality of its own, independent of the revelation of God in Jesus Christ.

Now I can't say I fully understand that, but something in me loves the fact that, in Jesus, God lays claim on all of our humanity. And he does so to give us what we long for and need. A true life.

One of the most attributed wisdom sayings of Jesus employs the concept of us needing not just a patch-up job, but a new garment:

> No one sews a patch of unshrunk cloth on an old garment. Otherwise, the new piece will pull away from the old, making the tear worse.
>
> *(Mark 2:21)*

Jesus offers this new cloth, which is his own humanity. In the light of his life, which is lived for us, he bids us give up our patchwork lives and take on his seamlessness. This isn't easy; many of us have worked really hard at the stitching. But our coverings are hostile to the integrated life he wants to give to us.

The wonderful creation poems in Genesis 3 tell how the first action of Adam and Eve after they became aware of their sin was to sew together pieces of fig leaves to cover their shame. Since those days we have constantly tried to sew together odd-fitting pieces to cover our lives. We are, all of us, in different fashions and with great or lesser skill, adept in making for ourselves coverings. The irony is then when one comes among us who lived a seamless life, he is stripped naked by us, and so takes the shame we try to hide. But time and time again then, as now, he bids us lay down our basic and sometimes fairly sophisticated patchwork lives, our repair jobs, the secret bits of our garments, the hidden pockets no one else knows anything about, and let ourselves be accepted and loved and reconstructed by him.

Jesus' humanity is the shining example of this God-shaped life, as he lives without contradiction, without compartmentalisation, without fracture. For example, he practises what he preaches. We've talked in the past of the boundaries that are important to have in ministry, and of course we need healthy lives, especially when it comes to our family. But a couple of years ago one of the teenagers at church was having such a hard time at home she came to live in our house. On her first night I nearly sent her packing, as she said that what she was most interested to see was whether I was a different person at home from who I was at church. I didn't want that level of scrutiny. I didn't want to be found out. I didn't want the glaring contradictions that my wife and children could justifiably raise against me to be seen by anyone who wasn't my flesh.

But Jesus was different. That is one of the reasons I am so drawn to him; not because I am like him, but because he is so different. What he tells others to do, he does himself; forgiveness, turning the other cheek, blessing those who persecute you, praying for your enemies, accepting the outsider. He lives seamlessly. Certainly not effortlessly. My philosopher friend, the seventeen-year-old Michael Lynch, poses a question we all struggle with when he asks, 'Why is it harder to be real than to be fake?'

Jesus lives life really, truly, deeply in his humanity because he is in step with the Spirit. Here again we need a rewiring of our brains. Rather than being anti-matter, the Holy Spirit enables us, to realise what we can be. Why should we be surprised at this? Was not the Spirit breathed into the first flesh that humans might live? Was it not the Spirit who enabled Jesus to be conceived, upheld and live his life at each turn for God? He turned aside from temptation because he was strengthened by the Spirit; he understood what was required of him in each situation because of his aliveness to the Spirit; he chose to suffer and give his life up for others because of the vibrancy of the Spirit in his life.

A little while back I mentioned a recent prominent leader boasting that he was bi-locational. His visitations to heaven enabled him, he claimed, to hear God's voice. I should have stood and sung the first and second verses of my favourite hymn:

> This is my father's world, and to my listening ears,
> all nature sings, and round me rings the music of the spheres …
> This is my father's world, the birds their carols raise,
> the morning light, the lily white, declare their Maker's praise.
> This is my Father's world: He shines in all that's fair,
> In the rustling grass I hear Him pass;
> he speaks to me everywhere.
>
> (*Maltbie D. Babcock*)

It might be rather simplistic, but the implications of this on our humanity, on this life of ours, couldn't be greater. So let's consider culture. My broad brushstroke take on it is that amongst the major world religions Christianity is unique because it does not carry a culture which it is bound to. Consider Islam: of course there are different expressions of the faith, but on the whole, the faith of Islam carries with it a culture – whether it be dress or language. All Muslim prayer happens in Arabic wherever it takes place in the world. The words of the Koran are read in Arabic. Hinduism, Sikhism and Buddhism carry with them cultures in terms of an affinity to a particular land or way of doing things and rituals done in a certain way throughout the world. Judaism (certainly in what is commonly called its orthodox form) carries with it specific dress and dietary requirements and particular ways of doing things. Christianity has no such culture. It looks different in different places.

Is it any wonder that from the earliest years Christian faith has looked different in each culture it has been part of? (I'm with Karl Barth on not being comfortable with calling Christianity a religion – I'm sure he will be thrilled.) Within a generation Greek Christianity looked different from Roman Christianity,

Ethiopian faith differed from Egyptian faith. Of course there were many skirmishes around this, but since the Council of Jerusalem decided you could follow Christ and not follow Judaism, Christians have spoken, written and read Jesus' words in their own mother tongue. I'd like to think that it's what we believe about incarnation and the Spirit that enables the faith to look different in every setting, with a shared universal common-ality of the tenets of the faith but a intensely local way of working out how to live them. God never works in generalities, slogans or formulas. The Spirit always has an address and does particular things in particular places. The following is an extract from the second-century letter of Diognetius describing Christianity in that period;

> Christians are indistinguishable from other men either
> by nationality, language or customs. They do not inhabit
> separate cities of their own, or speak a strange dialect, or
> follow some outlandish way of life. Their teaching is not
> based upon reveries inspired by the curiosity of men.
> Unlike some other people, they champion no purely
> human doctrine. With regard to dress, food and manner
> of life in general, they follow the customs of whatever
> city they happen to be living in, whether it is Greek or
> foreign.

Now you don't need me to point out to you, Nick, that the relationship between Christianity and the culture it is part of is one that we can do no more than skim the surface of. But can we not at least agree that discerning the relationship and the interac-tion between the two is a vital exercise if we are to truly live out an incarnated, seamless faith? Our faith needs to be lived out, not in some supernatural realm, but in the fabric of our lives.

In my last seminar before I left theological college to be ordained, two of my favourite teachers were together. I was writing down every word they were saying. One asked the other: 'What one piece of advice would you give these people who are about to be ordained?' The professor thought and waited for what seemed like too long, then he said something which has become a motto to my ministry:

> Never become a professional. Never second-guess God. Never enter a room and think you know already what God would have you be or say or pray. Never assume you know what word you should bring, what prayer you should pray, what support you should give. It will be different for each situation. Be alive to him.

Friends of ours came round the other year and in the first batch of conversation in the kitchen I was, I confess, a bit distracted. I apologise if I have ever done it to you too. Anyhow that afternoon there were a couple of calls I hadn't made, so I was trying to text surreptitiously, and it will come as no surprise to you that the kids were a bit hyper. After ten minutes my friend Steve (he's a consultant psychiatrist, as if that's going to give him much insight) looked me in the eye and said:

> I have been here now for ten minutes and you are doing what you always do. You try and do so many other things, and that means you aren't really here. We have driven all the way from Oxford and it is rather rude of you not to give me your full attention. And, what's more, this is a fairly regular pattern of your behaviour whenever we are around you.

Speak your mind, Steve, why don't you?

I had that surgey feeling I used to get when I had been found out during a primary school assembly and was made to stand up in front of the whole school. It's the kind of feeling in which I think I might wet myself. I put my phone down and concentrated.

I can't remember much of the rest of the night. In the following days, in an attempt to justify myself, I shared the conversation with some close friends at church, in that kind of 'can-you-believe-what-this-guy-said-to-me-isn't-itoutrageous-I-am-sure-you-will-agree-now-tell-me-i-never-do it' kind of way. And they all said that I regularly walked off mid-conversation with them.

A few days later Steve sent me a postcard. The picture was of a big red 'B', inside the loops of which were the words 'Wherever you are, be there.'

A desire to live an integrated life requires me to take where I am and who I am with the upmost seriousness. I often find myself giving God the excuse that I would be a fairly good Christian if it wasn't for everyone else around me and all the pressures that I feel under. That I would be a fairly on-fire Christian if it wasn't for how tired I was because the kids insist on waking up before six a.m. every morning, if I had more time to pray, if I didn't have the annoying habits I have, and if I had an amazingly-built beautiful chapel for my own personal use. Oh, and a quiet day every week.

But it is precisely in my life as it is now that God calls me to follow. *In Making All Things New* Henri Nouwen wrote:

> Jesus does not respond to our worry-filled way of living by saying that we should not be so busy with worldly affairs. He does not try to pull us away from the many events, activities and people that make up our lives. He does not tell us that what we do is unimportant, valueless or useless, nor does he suggest that we should withdraw from our involvement in the world and live quiet, restful lives removed from the struggles of the world.

> Jesus response to our worry-filled lives is quite different. He asks us to shift the point of gravity, to relocate the centre of our attention, to change our priorities.

My wrong assumption is too often that I could best follow Jesus in some other life, some other place, some other church. But it is in this life that he calls me to live and follow and glorify him. Living for God in a way that is full-on, vibrant, on fire and real isn't simply possible under laboratory conditions, or in California. It's not over there that God would best use me, it's here. We need to take our lives seriously as the raw materials God uses to show his glory and usher in his Kingdom. Do you see, Nick? That's the problem I have with the aching gap you feel between your routine life and what you think God really wants you to live – it's as if you think God's fully filled life for you would have none of the day-to-day reality about it.

But you and I and all of us who seek to follow Christ should take where we are and who we are with far more seriously than we do. There are many things I might face which feel un-ideal. There are things that I feel mitigate against me living more closely for God. There are things which are hard and if I could be without them, I most certainly would. But for too long, I wondered if by just making four or five changes I might live the most wonderfully empowered and profound Christian life; if I was able to move beyond these few struggles or hardships or mundanities, then I would rise on wings like eagles. Then that prophecy so beloved in the 1990s might be true for me; I might be able to be one of those birds that just catch the thermals and glide rather than flapping my wings as if my life depended on it.

But this must be rejected. The Christian life is not improved by fantasies. It is in this life, in these hard choices, facing these things we face, that we can fully live for God. We cannot just wait for ideal conditions; we must not give in to the temptation to believe that life would be easier and spiritual life more real if we weren't in the life we live. Look how un-ideal Jesus' life was; who he was surrounded by, how he was misunderstood, how he suffered, the hard choices he had to make. No, as Eugene Peterson says in *Christ Plays in Ten Thousand Places* (everyone should have a copy, and read it):

> It turns out the hardest thing is to believe that God's work – this dazzling creation, this cascade of blessings – is all being worked out in and under the conditions of our humanity: at picnics and around dinner tables, in conversations and while walking along the roads, in puzzled questions and homely stories, with blind

beggars and suppurating lepers, at weddings and
funerals. Everything Jesus does and says takes place
within the limits and conditions of our humanity, no
fireworks. No special effects.

It is, says Peterson, the devil's work to seduce us into believing
that Christian formation can only truly take place as we construct
a utopia, an ideal place where we can live totally and without
inhibition or interference the good and blessed and righteous life.
This is the theme of much of Peterson's writing.

All this is not just to baptize the current situations in which we
live as being exactly what should be happening. There is a
credibility gap we need to hold out on between where we find
ourselves and where God might be calling us to reach for. Our
reach should always extend our grasp. God always longs to bring
transformation and difference. But what God longs to bring us is
possible in these lives that we lead. It doesn't involve us morphing
into different people, or having different personalities or bank
accounts.

It is on our knees in prayer that the seams of our lives get
woven together. You know I have never claimed to find prayer
easy, but I do know it's essential. Here we bring all we are before
all that God is, and allow him to reformulate us and it. There are a
couple of essential ways this happens, and they both pick up on
themes we have already nudged against.

The first is presence.

The outgoing Archbishop of Canterbury, Dr Rowan Williams, who has brains the size of Birmingham and a relationship
with God I would covet if coveting wasn't ruled out by the
commandments, was asked in a interview with the *Daily Telegraph*
in 2002 what advice he could give readers on prayer. He offered
the following:

> Somebody once said that the deepest problem in prayer
> is often not the absence of God but the absence of me.
> I'm not actually there. My mind is everywhere. So take
> a few deep breaths, use a simple formula like the

Orthodox, 'Lord Jesus Christ, Son of God, have mercy', and sense in that that the line is anchored somewhere in the depths.

I can pray great prayers without really being present. You know, in those prayer meetings in which you pray prayers for the sake of the other people listening. I fell asleep in the middle of a prayer I prayed the other week. And the other day I got to the end of my prayer, which had got lots of agreement from others during the prayer, said 'Amen' and realised I couldn't remember a thing I had just prayed. There have been some brilliant movements in prayer that have happened over these last few years, offering a real engagement for people in these wonderful mysteries and creatively, deeply, and wonderfully exploring the treasure chest of the ancient resources available to us in the faith. Yet sometimes, just sometimes, it can feel as if my lack of concentration is being pandered to. Sometimes our really creative prayer meetings can feel like play meetings, and I wonder if it might not be good for us every once in a while not to be offered interactive and exciting prayer stations with sand, candles, paint, clay, newspaper, video, plasticine or string, but just a kneeler.

However I do it, in prayer I am called to come before God. To be there. To be present for him, to him, before him. And when I do, I realise he has been present to me all the time. So, as helpful as other people's experience can be, and as much as we can learn from other Christians, I wonder if importing techniques and practices from outside really get us to where we need to be.

The second is participation.

Prayer holds out for something different. Prayer is an exercise which we embark on to see change. And I can't be doing with the nonsense that says prayer just changes me. That is to reduce prayer to some self-reflective, self-help tool. No, true prayer holds out for something different from God. It's here that we feel the tension the most, of being where and how we are, and longing to be where and how we could be.

The most helpful way I have been given of thinking about this is from Eugene Peterson's *The Contemplative Pastor*, and involves a quick lesson in English grammar. No, stick with me on this one, I know it doesn't sound great, but it really does work in the end. Basically there are three different 'voices' that ancient language used to use: the active, the passive and the middle. In such a scheme of things, let's say you were getting or giving advice. In the active voice you would say, 'I counsel my friend' – it's when you initiate an action. In the passive voice you might say, 'I receive counsel' – there you receive the action another initiates. But in the middle voice you would say 'I take counsel'. This middle one introduces an idea that I take part in something I didn't start; that the initiative for it started somewhere else, with someone else, but that I actively play a part in it. This is Christian prayer. Prayer which we join in with, but in which the action is begun by God. It's not some notion that we give God ideas for things he didn't already have, or that we make him do things he needs persuading to do. But neither is it just a passive receiving of a pre-set course of action. No, it is involving ourselves actively in the work of God, which brings a different outcome than would have been the case had we not have prayed.

In prayer, then, we locate ourselves in the real conditions of our lives and we hold out for something different. This 'something different' is the work of God, which doesn't begin with us, but with his loving kindness is initiated in our lives by him, and into which we join and participate. The doors are always open for us all.

The last word must go to one of the most influential and seismic saints of our day. Eugene Peterson served at the same church for some twenty-five years. He taught spiritual theology at Regent College. He has written over thirty books, and his contemporary language version of the Bible, called *The Message*, has brought the words of Scripture alive to many of us. Bono so loved it he asked Peterson to spend a weekend with the band when they were in Chicago. Peterson said no. He still had three chapters of Isaiah to translate. (The interviewer said, 'Yeah, but it was U2', and Peterson said 'Yes, but it was Isaiah.') In a recent interview published in *Subversive Spirituality*, he was asked the following question. I still have to pick myself up off the floor whenever I read his answer.

Interviewer: If you knew you were giving your last sermon or message, what would be some of your themes?

Eugene Peterson: I think I would want to talk about the things that are immediate and ordinary. In the kind of world we live in, the primary way that I can get people to be aware of God is to say, 'Who are you going to have breakfast with tomorrow, and how are you going to treat that person?' I want to pay attention to what people are doing, and help them do it in acts of faith and prayer. I guess I'd want to say, 'Go home and be good to your wife. Treat your children with respect. And do a good job at whatever you've been given to do.'

Seamless.

Nick, I wonder whether you might be more in God's zone if you didn't fly around the world chasing the latest faith fads for a year? If you didn't assume God's agenda was just for the big, the bold and the obvious? If you weren't always looking somewhere else for what God was doing, but attuned yourself to your present for his presence? If you didn't isolate God to just the 'spiritual' zone? But if you took your life seriously as the place God would show his glory?

Imagine, Nick, what it would look like not to live a different life, but to live your life differently. To live it not with a restlessness to escape the mundanity of life, but to find God right there in the middle of it all. Imagine not having to import God's effects from somewhere beyond the horizon, but being alive to see them before your eyes. Imagine living seamlessly – all of your life before all of God.

Keep wearing those shirts,

Chris

6

Ask

To Phil

Phil was one of those students at theological college who were always ready with the answers. He loved being asked questions because he had index cards with three-point replies, backed up with specific Bible verses. And he had shoes that made a metal click when he walked. He was part of a group known as the Sound Crowd. Naturally they took the name as a compliment. We used it with a snigger.

Although they treated those of us on the outside of the group with a bit of suspicion, they were kind people. Phil went, like the rest of the Sound Crowd, to an established and respected play-it-with-a-straight-bat kind of church. In subsequent years he has become quite a star there.

The church is a super-sure-of-itself church, conservative and fairly 'us against the world'. They always seems to have a prepared response for everything: no question can fox them, because they know the answers already. The sermons often have five points beginning with 'P'. They take a hard line on all questions of morality – hell is talked about as a place of eternal suffering for those who haven't said a prayer giving their hearts to Jesus, and other churches are taken down. It feels very controlled and unemotional, very rational and logical, quite clinical and pre-set. It's clear who's in and who's out.

This letter makes contact again and simply poses question after question.

Dear Phil,

It's been some time since I was in touch (about twelve years). There's lots I could tell you but I wonder whether I can really get to the point of this letter. There are simply a few questions I would love to ask.

Do you not think that questions are sometimes more important, more telling, more revealing than answers?

Is not one of the most fascinating things about Jesus that he asked so many questions?

Do you think that sometimes we might get on better talking about him as the question rather than the answer?

The longest set of questions in the Bible are those God asks of Job. My particular favourites are:

> Can you bring forth the constellations in their seasons or lead out the Bear with its cubs? (38:32)

> Do you know when the mountain goats give birth? (39:1)

> Can you pull in Leviathan with a fishhook, or tie down its tongue with a rope?

I don't know the answers to any of those questions. What questions does God/would God ask of you? What do you think he would ask of me?

Do you think God sometimes asks us questions because we need to sit with the question, rather than come up with the answer?

> *Oh my soul … be prepared for him who knows how to ask questions.*
>
> (*T. S. Eliot*)

When you think of God do you think he is static or moving?

Does the whole gift of life not reduce you to tears?

Considering the size of the universe, how small do you feel?

How well do you think we represent that in our claims for knowing the exact truth?

Do you think all truth is God's truth?

Has God breathed life into everybody?

What is that sense that everyone feels at a big U2/Mumford/Elbow/Matt Greener gig? What if it's God?

What is that goodness people know when they commit themselves sacrificially to another, when they pour their lives out for the sake of other people? What if that's God?

What of those, of any faith and none, who cry out to something beyond themselves? Is that God?

What of that sense of a 'vertigo of gladness' before a beautiful piece of art, overlooking a view, hearing Mozart? Could that be God?

Do you think that, if we looked closely, we might see the shape of the cross as a pattern, a fractal, a rhythm that exists in all faiths, all cultures and all people?

Do you think it could be possible that God might meet all people in these patterns of death and resurrection, whether or not they know they are part of his work in Jesus?

What if God is doing all sorts of things, in a myriad of ways, but because we're blinkered and have a prescribed grid for understanding him, we have determined it can't be him, when actually it is?

> *The Bible is a book which gives us more questions than answers.*
>
> (*Anon*)

Do you think an approach to scripture which takes it all at face value and uses words like inerrancy and infallibility is, in fact, unscriptural?

Does it matter if Jonah wasn't a historical character?

Do you ever wonder why your take on scripture seems to find everyone else – Pentecostals, Charismatics, Catholics, Liberals, Emerging types – in the wrong, and you in the clear?

Do you ever wonder if your take on scripture might not be more like self-justification than a correct reading?

Do you think we might do wonderfully poetic passages an injustice by reducing them to a five-point sermon with each point beginning with P?

What about the fact that this book was written to be read out loud, that no one could have had any idea that individuals would have their own personal copy? Should we pin so much on an individual's ability to own their own copy of the Bible and read it for 30 minutes every day?

What about the fact that the majority of Christians who have ever lived have been illiterate?

Do you ever think we rob scripture of its power by reducing it to a few simple steps?

Do you think some people have settled for a relationship with their Bibles rather than with God?

Do you think the Bible was given to answer all the problems and questions we have in today's world?

> *The intolerance that has spread over the world with the advent of Christianity is one of its most curious features.*
>
> (*Bertrand Russell*)

Do you think we in the church have the same obsession with sex that the 'world' has?

Are you aware of how far many of the Old Testament heroes would fall short of a 'Christian' sexual morality?

Is it possible for someone to be a full-on Christian and be in a same sex-covenanted and committed relationship?

Can you see that a gay person who loves Jesus and finds themselves deeply in love with a member of the same sex would want to give themselves to things we applaud as Christian principles: faithfulness, commitment, sacrifice, and love?

St Paul tells the Christians in Corinth that if they burn with passion they are to marry. What should gay people do if they burn with passion?

Have we not refigured what scripture says about divorce and remarriage?

Do you think our children and grandchildren might look back at our generation of the church and be perplexed by our stance on homosexuality?

Do you think it might be compared with slavery in a generation or two?

Have I failed the 'sound' litmus test for being willing to ask the above questions, which I myself don't completely know the answer to?

Would you give a person in a gay relationship communion? Would you give an arms dealer communion? What about someone who was a gossip? What about someone who fiddles their taxes? Whose table is it?

It's clearly the case that Jesus spent much of his time with those who had been sidelined by mainstream religion; how do you think he would interact with gay people today? How would this differ from the approach the church takes?

Are you aware that the general atmosphere that pervades the church is anti-sex? Does that make a reading of the Song of Songs rather embarrassing?

Are you aware that the Bible clearly bans lending money on interest (calling it usury)? Why we have reversed that one?

> *My humanity is bound up in yours, for we can only be human together.*
>
> (*Desmond Tutu*)

Do you think God is found among the poor?

What responsibility do we have to the millions of children who are born as HIV/AIDS orphans? What about those who have no clean water? What about those who will die of malaria because the western drug companies charge too high a price for drugs and inoculations?

What does turning the other cheek look like when it involves the Taliban?

If it's easier for a camel to pass through the eye of a needle than for a rich man to enter the kingdom of heaven, why do we spend so much time making it easy for them and treating them as if their presence is more valuable than anyone else's?

If we all gave all our money away do you think people outside the church might find our faith easier to believe?

How can we make all sorts of contextual caveats and gymnastics around what scripture says about money but not about homosexuality?

How did the church of Jesus Christ get on this side of the wealthy divide?

Why is Christianity is associated with power and authority?

> *Men never do evil so completely and cheerfully as when they do it from a religious conviction.*
>
> (*Blaise Pascal*)

How did a faith whose founder didn't have a house, or a wage, or any political power end up with all this?

In the light of what Jesus says to the religious leaders at the time, what do you think he would say to the church today? And not just other churches, but the church you are part of?

What do you think the church would do with Jesus today if he did come among us and speak his mind?

Have we made Jesus look a bit too much like us?

When he said, 'I tell you, you will do even greater things than these,' what on earth did he mean? Why don't we see any big healings? Why is it always colds, sprains and the like?

Would we recognise him if he came among us?

Do you think the life the church lives witnesses to the life that is in God?

Is God really present among us? What would it look like if he was?

Why are churches and their members so mean to those they disagree with?

How is it that my friend, who is a phenomenal preacher, has had death threats from other Christians for things he has said about God?

Is God in the emerging church?

Are you aware how irrelevant church is to the majority of this nation's young people? Is that not a sin?

What do you think the church will look like in a hundred years' time?

> Standing on a London street corner, G. K. Chesterton was approached by a reporter:
>
> 'Sir, I understand that you recently became a Christian. May I ask you one question?'
>
> 'Certainly,' replied Chesterton.
>
> 'If the risen Christ suddenly appeared at this very moment and stood behind you, what would you do?'
>
> Chesterton looked at the reporter squarely in the eye and said, 'He is.'

Have we sanitised Jesus' death?

Can the mystery of the Son of God dying it really be explained by all those long technical words?

Is it just me, or does 'propitiation' really flatten the power of this most loving event?

If we had had a video camera trained on the entrance of his tomb, what do you think we would have seen?

Did Jesus need sleep during the forty days of his resurrection?

Why did some people still doubt even when they saw him?

How is Jesus present to those who are suffering?

When Jesus entered Jerusalem we are told he was weeping; what do you think he might weep over today?

What do you think he thinks of different denominations and those who claim to follow him?

What do you think he is praying for you today?

Do you think there is anything in the idea that no one could look in God's face and live because no one could bear to see the sorrow in his face, as we constantly reject his love?

Eskimo: 'If I did not know about God and sin, would I go to hell?'

Priest: 'No, not if you did not know.'

Eskimo: 'Then why did you tell me?'

(*Annie Dillard*)

Do you think more people will be saved than not?

Is there any contradiction in your mind between hell as a place of burning torment and a God of love?

Can God really be an eternal torturer?

How come I knew you would square that circle?

Do you ever think that the way we tell it makes people not particularly interested in salvation? How can that be?

Do you think you will be surprised at who you meet in the new heaven and new earth?

Why isn't grace irresistible?

You know I ask myself all these questions and more?

To be honest I would have loved to have heard your answers. But I would have been more interested in the questions you wanted to ask me.

Chris

7

Why?

To Tommy

Tommy was my nephew by marriage, the only child of my wife's brother and his wife. They tried for years for him. He was the apple of their eye.

In February 2010, three days before his first birthday, in a freak accident he was struck by a falling lamppost while asleep in his pushchair in a London street. His head took the full force of the blow.

I will never forgot the smells, sounds and feelings of the following three days, beginning with the phone call from the scene of the accident: the constant updates as we tore into London, the sight of the air ambulance arriving at the hospital, the intensive care unit, the wires and tubes and pumps and beeps, the head-shaking (this can't be happening,) the helplessness, the gut-wrenching news of hopelessness from the doctors.

He died two days later.

In those two days before he died, while he was on a life-support machine, members of the family sat with him, stroking his hand and talking to him. The first time I sat with him I was unable to say anything. On subsequent times I asked him to pass on a message to Jesus. As a way of dealing with grief, a friend of mine who is a psychologist suggested I wrote a letter to Tommy, expressing my feelings and thoughts.

Dearest Tommy,

The only flimsy glimmer of comfort has come from the fact that they told us you hadn't suffered. For the rest of us, particularly your parents, the unbearable suffering in these first weeks has redefined and reframed us.

Recently we were just sitting round the table drinking tea, when your dad put his mug down, stared into the area of space that so much of our gaze has recently been drawn to and summed it up: 'The world has changed. For ever.'

My guess is that there are only a handful of events in our lives which truly rearrange us, redefine us and re-form us. These are the events which split time into a before and after, which act as a benchmark for anything that can be said, brought, or hoped for, and which shape our everyday lives in both involuntary and voluntary ways. Our world is never the same again.

It's a strange thing writing a letter to you. Obviously it won't be read by you. But I guess it's for those who have had life redefined by this tragedy. But not to address you, to exclude you and the events of your death from my horizon, would be to ignore how your life has refigured us. But I wanted to set out how things have changed for all of us: in loving you, in feeling pain, in finding solace in community, and within it all sensing the presence of the one familiar with sufferings, who meets us in the depths of our agony and repaints the scene with glimmers of golden light. This is how things are never going to be the same.

We all sensed from the outset that the time we were given with you in the intensive care unit on floor 3 of King's College Hospital in London was grievously unique. We felt the weight of each second and the lightness of each hour. The air connecting our time and eternity seemed all too thin; the distance between heaven and earth felt both tangibly near and an aching ocean apart; our sense of helplessness was brutally apparent and over-whelmingly obvious.

But we gave you up with thanks to God, because you changed our worlds.

You had come to mean so much to so many of us. For your parents you meant so much before you were even conceived, for they had longed for your life for years. For those of us who toasted your expected arrival some six months before your birth, on Father's Day 2008, as your flushed Dad popped the joyous news of your conception, our hope in you was never disappointed; you were more to us than we had imagined. For those who met you, family and friends – to each of us you meant something indefinable.

You were such a wonderful boy.

When you came round to our house, for what your Dad would call 'Tommy time', you would hold court – a difficult thing to do in a house of three girls themselves so big on personality – but you would somehow capture the attention and affection in the room and give it back.

You were a boy who was loved and you knew it. In your life, your too-short life, there was not a day that you did not know love.

Loving people changes everyone involved. For your mother and father this is part of the most harrowing aspects of pain. The extent to which they are changed corresponds to the amount they loved you. And to be honest with you, it was total.

To your last moments your parents poured their love out on you. It was one of the greatest privileges in my life to be able to watch it, feel it and learn from it. In the hospital there were holy moments, where their actions in loving you took on sacramental weight. You lay motionless with tubes coming in and going out, wired up to beeping machines and pulsing monitors, and they sat holding you, stroking you, with their own excruciating comfort of no consequence. There they caressed you, cradled you and sang to you – on the one hand powerless to do anything yet so powerfully giving you everything. Sacred moments of seemingly unredeemable time.

They are changed because they loved you. There can be no return for them now. They poured their lives out on you. And such love expands our hearts and we are never the same. There is and can be no return – your parents are always your parents, your mummy and daddy, we are always your relatives, your friends. Loving you made us all better. It made life better. Love is never in vain. But loving you, this giving and receiving, 'shifts the boundaries of our being'.

The world has changed because we loved you.

But it is precisely this love that makes it all so difficult. Not having you to hold, to tangibly, physically love, makes the world feel flat and empty, meaningless and bare, trivial and worn out.

Of course this love now changes the world of the past. It makes nothing easier, but everything harder. The joy of good memories becomes a source of pain; the importance of remembering increases the agony. There are regrets and so many what-ifs, the dull ache of loss and the heaviness of grief.

My sense is that we all need to truly engage with the desperation of this: we need to feel it; not push it down, not put a brave face on it, and certainly not expect that we can carry on in the same way that we did before. We refuse the many escapes from death and grief. We are embraced by its rawness, which now defines everything.

In the days after your death a book by a man who had lost his teenage son began to make new sense. Nicholas Wolterstorff's son Eric died in a climbing accident, and in *Lament for a Son* he describes the terrible transformation of his life by Eric's death. He talks of the choice to embrace the pain or to try and ride roughshod over it. Although embrace is the wrong word. It makes it sound as if we have control of it. We don't. But we can choose either to be embraced (or is it engulfed?) by the pain, or to push it aside. He makes the hardest choice; he refuses to 'look away from Eric dead'.

For him the future is so painful:

> It is the neverness that is so painful. Never again to be here with us – never to sit at our table, never to travel with us, never to laugh with us, never to cry with us, never to embrace us as he leaves for school … All the rest of our lives we must live without him. Only our death can stop the pain of his death.

It feels so unrepairable. Because it is so unrepairable.

It's that 'neverness' which he talks about which creates the vertigo. A vertigo that we sense we will never be rid of. The suspense of it all, for we know that what we want is precisely what we can never get.

The world has changed because we mourn a loss, and not just our loss, but your loss. The 'neverness' of the things isn't primarily about us but about you. As one of our girls said when we told them, 'But Daddy, he will never be able to grow up.' It's the things we anticipate for you which will never be, the potential that was never realised. So we wonder about things we will never know:

- What would your voice have sounded like?
- What about your singing voice?
- What would your face have looked like through the different stages of growth?
- What would have been the gait of your walk?
- What would have been the name of your first school?
- What subjects would you have thrived in at in school?
- What would faith have meant to you?
- What would your friends have enjoyed about you?
- How would we have celebrated your eighteenth birthday?
- Would you have reminded us of your mother? Of your father?
- Would you have married?

We feel the world has changed because of this pain, this sadness. Of course there are questions to ask and whisper, to shout and communicate by the mere shaking of our heads.

We think of times past and wonder at our carefree natures and outlooks. We wonder whether our eyes will ever adjust to this darkness. A mother I listened to the other day, talking of the recent death of her daughter, said: 'I will never enjoy anything ever again.'

Yet we remember that your world never turned bad. You didn't know suffering and pain. A true facing of suffering and pain washes up in its wake so many questions, which need to find some stillness in order to be asked. Even if they only rebound in the silence.

Wolterstorff rehearses question after question:

Can sadness be relieved, or can one only pass it by, very slowly?

Was I deluded in believing that in God the question shouted out by the wounds of the world has its answer? Am I deluded in believing that some day I will know the answer?

Why don't you raise my son now? Why must your conquest of sin and death and suffering be so achingly slow?

Why 'blessed are those who mourn?' Why does he hail the world's mourners? Why isn't love-without-suffering the meaning of things? Why is suffering-love the meaning?

Why does God endure his suffering?

Why does he not at once relieve his agony by relieving ours?

How can we thank God for suffering's yield while asking for its removal? How do I sustain my 'no' to my son's early death while accepting with gratitude the opportunity of becoming what otherwise I would never be?

It can be in the times of quiet where it can be hardest. A young man who sailed round the world recollected that it wasn't the storms that were most terrifying, but the motionless calm of a windless day on the wide ocean. On some days it feels as if there has never been any wind, and there will never be anything other than this eerie, unsettling stillness.

It's in such calm that we learn to lament. Lamenting is an ancient discipline. It's not a morbid complaint, a hopeless shrug of the shoulders, but a willingness to engage with the pain of this changed world, where the best way through suffering is to suffer it, where grief is something you don't get over, but go through. Michael Card describes this in *A Sacred Sorrow: Reaching Out to God in the Lost Language of Lament*.

Nearly half of all the psalms are laments. Of course you wouldn't know that from most of the songs we sing in church, but we need those songs that speak of the pain of our reality. And we never sing them alone.

I remember one candlelight evening spent with a dear friend of mine. He was sharing what had helped him most in the years in which he had gone through a rollercoaster of emotions as his son, born with a serious heart abnormality, had been in and out of hospital for tests, surgery, bypass after bypass. It wasn't the declarations that he would be healed. It wasn't the vista of a frothy, grinning, pain-free life on the other side of the fence. It was, what he called, 'the community of the suffering'. These are those, he explained, who are not vociferous in their claims, nor definite in their pronouncements; in fact often they are tentative and they are never simplistic. But they are present when they see a fellow sufferer.

Here in this suffering-changed world we, the community of the suffering, offer each other compassion as balm for the wounds. We pour out love, trust, kindness, compassion in giving and receiving. The world is changed for those who suffer not simply because of pain, but because we never know how much we really believe anything until its truth or falsehood become a matter of life and death to us. And so our world changes because we find in this community of suffering a depth and height and breadth of relating that we never knew.

And we realise that, while in our western world we do everything to shield ourselves from suffering at every turn, in suffering we become part of the majority in the world. For the community of the suffering spans the world.

It has not been difficult for us to give love to your parents in their suffering, for they give it so freely to so many. The presence of so many people surrounding your parents brought huge comfort and support: members of the local community, the local church family, friends and those who just found your death touching them deeply. The world changes when we bear this suffering together.

So together as a community we stood, we bowed our heads, we remembered, we grieved, we lamented, and we continue to insist that lessons are learnt so that other people's worlds do not have to change as ours have because of such an avoidable incident.

But the world has not changed simply because one who we so loved has died; it has not just changed because of the pain and sadness this suffering has brought and what we have found in each other, it has changed because this all happens before the face of God. And God constantly and tenaciously makes the difference.

I know there are those for whom the event of your death makes it harder, much harder to believe. Of course, bringing God into it can intensify the suffering. It is an event that changes the landscape and horizon in which we talk about God.

I remember reading a book on the holocaust and being confronted with a shocking line, which went something like: 'nothing now can be said of God which couldn't be said within range of the smell of burning children'. For many of us nothing now should be said about God that can't be said in the wake of your tragic death.

This of course doesn't mean that everything we say must have some reference to this tragedy; rather that any talk of God or faith must be possible to say and believe, having experienced what we have experienced. I read the book of Job again in wonder at the wisdom of his three friends saying nothing for seven days, then failing miserably in their friendship when they open their mouths, because they tried to fit the suffering of Job into their previously constructed, neat patterns of belief.

The hardest of statements to bear are those which talked of this somehow being God's 'will' and us 'just' having to trust the sovereign God. They didn't seem to consider what the implications of such a belief might be; were they really suggesting that it was part of God's will for a lamppost to fall, not just anywhere, at any time, but on you, whereas half an inch either way would have made all the difference? Were they implying that God had mapped out that fatal route on that Tuesday morning? That God let such an unnecessary, meaningless, tragic event shatter lives? Why would we, why would anyone, be drawn to such a God? Why would we worship such a God? Simply out of quaking fear that if we didn't turn in obedience we might be on the receiving end of some heinous indescribable act? It would be a response of stooping fear, given only out of desperate anxiety that a similar meaningless fate might be further meted out upon us.

No, in the light of what happened to you, Tommy I can't have any truck with talk of this being God's will for your life, or our lives.

Personally I can't envisage this tragedy fitting into your plans or being how it was supposed to be – it was a meaningless, futile accident which reveals the fragility of our lives.

Our faith must be able to have enough space in it for this event. Not to be made sense of – for that will never be – but simply to be an event that happened.

Nothing will ever be able to erase the sights and sounds, the smells and noises of those three days in the hospital. There we wept and groaned, we shook our heads in disbelief and we implored God to bring your life back from the brink.

I prayed every prayer I could think of, in every way I could think possible. I pleaded with God and bargained with him. I tried to convince him that he would get so much out of a miraculous healing now; imagine the lives that would be turned to him with such an intervention.

Our prayers weren't answered. We didn't get what we wanted. But what we did get was God's presence. There in the valley of the shadow of death, as we baptised you on the Tuesday night, as we prayed the following night, there came among us the divine man, a man of sorrows and one familiar with suffering.

This is a God who is not a lever-pulling, capricious and random tyrant. Before such a deity we would shake in fear, for who knows what he would let happen to us. No, because Jesus defines who God is, this is one who is on this side of our pain. Always with the suffering, not causing it.

Here the balm comes from faith which doesn't beat us into submission before a shocking God who enacts incalculable suffering upon people, but one who enters into the pain of this world, where time and time again the mystery of suffering knocks us out of shape. The true God doesn't heal our pain, except through being infected with it.

Sometimes I can still hear (no that's not the right word, *feel*) the sounds of your last days on earth. The sobs which involuntarily came and echoed through the fibres of the corridor of the ICU as we fell against the wall in agony at the nightmare which was all too real, were from the deepest parts of our being. Those low tremors of grief twisted the most tender part of us.

Numerous times in his life we are told Jesus was moved in this place, the deepest place, the lowest chasm inside him. The sounds of the plates of the earth shifting and grinding. These fractures of pain hurt, and things should not be this way. God comes to us and feels what we feel. What if his presence is known more in the suffering and agony, than in the triumph?

Some weeks after your death, we came to the edge of Holy Week. A week which crescendoes (or is it a diminuendo, to silence?) to Good Friday – an event which rearranges, which redefines not just our world, not just the faithful's world, but the whole world.

For here, instead of explaining our suffering, God shares it. Through the prism of tears we see a suffering God, a wounded healer. Here a son dies a tragic, unnecessary death, through no fault of his own. Here a son cries out in the agony of being forsaken by the God whose love and goodness he had lived each of his moments, for each of his days. And a father watches in agony as his son shares and bears the pain of the world. And so Jesus' deepest cries resound in the gut-wrenching involuntary groans of despair around the world: in Darfur, in Kabul, in Northern Somalia, in Syria, in the ICU ward at King's College Hospital. And with the sound of these cries comes to us a realisation that we are not alone in our forsakenness. The suffering God is present.

This presence sometimes brings miraculous healing. Your death, Tommy, has not stopped me praying for that in others. But that is up to God, rather than to my technique or formula. Healing is the work of God's hands, but what we most need is his very presence, God's very self. And on his cross the world changes as God enters in.

Yet there is more, so much more. For following the suffering cross is an empty cross. Then come the next day, Holy Saturday, the longest of all days, a time suspended between despair and hope. And beyond that day the first day of the week, the Sunday marked by an empty tomb. And so this death and resurrection reveal one who knows that suffering, tragedy and even death, do not, will not, have the last word about life.

Not simply because here God is known. But because this Jesus comes through the pain, and opens it out into something we cannot make happen or manufacture ourselves. A life of the future. Resurrection. A creation healed, where all shall be well. Where tears are wiped away, suffering gone, everything made new. He changes the world, infects it with hope and rumours of resurrection and invites us to live this as true.

It is in the light of this resurrection that we can see your fulfilment. It is this seismic event which sews through this darkness an unquenchable thread of gold. A thread which some-times we manage to hold long enough in our hands to feel the lightness of, which murmurs into our imaginations and wonder-ings: hope. Hope of a time when all things are made new, when everything is fulfilled, when loved ones are reunited and when we meet again. For in life and death, in suffering and healing, in tragedy and chance, in frailty and strength we are loved, held and accompanied by one who we trust makes sense of it all.

So, Tommy, I pray not for you, for you are with our loving God, but for your parents and wider family and for all who bear the weight of you death, who are forever changed, that they may know, in the tumult of the storms and in the aching silence of the quiet windless day, the relentless love of God. That we would keep remembering and loving you and know God's balm in the love that holds you up and goes between us. And that we would know the presence of the wounded healer, the one familiar with suffering, holding us in our pain and drawing us to a world where all is remade. That we would know that he made our pain-drenched story his story, so we could know that his story is as true for us as it is for you, our dearest Tommy.

Until everything is made new,

Your uncle,

Chris

Note to reader: Tommy's parents have set up a charity, the Tommy Hollis Children's Fund, for the benefit of underprivileged, sick and orphaned children, and bereaved parents: www.tommyhol-lisfund.co.uk

8

Worship

To Gemma

Gemma is a Geordie who could persuade anyone to do anything. We met her over a decade ago, in the year before we moved to Reading. She then felt the tug of God and moved to begin the church with us. She is gregarious and brave, lighting up rooms and lives. After three years when we still didn't have any musicians at church she decided enough was enough, so she taught herself to play the guitar. When she had learnt three chords she became our official worship leader. When she learnt an extra three chords she found the whole Christian worship repertoire was open to her. Now she juggles coordinating the church's worshipping life, being a mother and managing Westy, her husband. We have monthly meetings where we will discuss the state of where we are at, and how we might get to where God might have us. This letter is to set an agenda for the future discussions she might have in helping the church find its way in the worship of the true God.

Dear Gemma,

I can't tell you how grateful I am for the sacrifices you have made to be part of this whole adventure. I know many times the lure of the North – the space, the people, the weather – has nearly snatched you from our grasp, but that one thing has kept you here. And that is this; your sense of calling to shape in these young people lives which are lived in worship to God. Your particular vocation has been to hold, urge, stimulate, stir up, prescribe and champion our corporate life before God, that we might give adequate response to him. And what we have seen emerge has been fitting. For God and for us. But in our monthly meeting we always talk about the 'more' that is there for us, the satisfied but unsatisfied sense that what we have tasted together of God is merely the beginnings. So this letter is an attempt to write the scope of the worshipping life of the church in large letters, widening the arc of the vision to somewhere beyond the horizon.

So let me say now that I know this is too big. But it feels it is worth aiming for. It feels an aspiration a little like Coca-Cola's aim of every house having a third tap at the sink running with Coke. But maybe if we aim at this, we might get to where we could be.

So I will set out worship as our primary Christian existence. Of course worship isn't about boundaried moments and slots of time, but about every moment in all time. Worship is our life before God; it is an orientation of the whole of our life to God. But if that is the general and the broad, it is directed, informed, and enabled in the particular, that is as the corporate body gather before the face of God. This instinct to worship is natural to us, but its formation and practice is something taught and learned, and this is one of the primary tasks of the church, to learn and teach this. In attending to this I will once again go on about the desire that worship is true to who God is, and that the very least we want to say about God as Christians is that God is Father, Son and Holy Spirit. The heart of true Trinitarian worship is encounter, and through the scriptural metaphor of the 'face' I will set out an idea of how we might conceive of describing this encounter. This isn't first and foremost a personal or private experience, but a corporate and communal one, and it is facilitated and realised in singing, openness and transformation. But as all this might seem like an exercise in imagination I will set forward, probably a bit too starkly, some of the barriers that stop us realising this; in particular stoicism (living on the level rather than in the highs and lows) and the worship 'industry' – an ugly term for a less than beautiful enterprise.

I recently read a book called *Teaching a Stone to Talk*, in which the author, Annie Dillard, tells the story of how, when she was on holiday, she decided to visit the church in the village. Her experience there that morning stirred her to write the following:

> Why do we people in churches seem like cheerful, brainless tourists on a packaged tour of the Absolute? On the whole, I do not find Christians, outside of the catacombs, sufficiently sensible of conditions. Does anyone have the foggiest idea what sort of power we so blithely invoke? Or, as I suspect, does not one believe a word of it? The churches are children playing on the floor with their chemistry sets, mixing up a batch of TNT to kill a Sunday morning. It is madness to wear ladies' straw hats and velvet hats to church; we should all be wearing crash helmets. Ushers should issue life preservers and signal flares. For the sleeping God may wake someday and take offence, or the waking God may draw us out to where we can never return.

While this seems rather stark, I find the polemic of it, the sense of a gauntlet being thrown, essential to weigh and hold, however heavy it feels. It is right for us to insist that worship is basic to our Christian existence. The theologian I rant on about more than any other, Karl Barth, wrote in *Church Dogmatics* that the first distinguishing mark of the Christian community was praise. There is an 'of course' about this. If God is God then praise is essential. In praise and worship it is clarified who we are and what we are for. Namely, God.

Praise and worship are a response to who we have learnt, heard, experienced, believed, hoped, lived, seen, shared and delighted in God to be. We affirm the most basic of truths; that we live before God's face and that he loves us. Everything has been brought into being by this God; everything is a freely given gift. And even more; he has made us for himself. As my professor, David Ford, wrote in *Praising and Knowing God*, worship is an attempt to cope with the abundance of God's love.

As the Church of Jesus Christ we are called primarily to attend to him. And to attend to him, not for ourselves, but for his own sake. Of course, the older we get, the more we realise we rarely if at all did anything from entirely pure motives, but in praise and worship our motives are refined and we come freely to give. This praise and worship is gratuitous, not for ourselves, but for God. It is not strictly necessary, nor can it be demanded of anyone. To insist on it or squeeze it from people is to misunderstand the most fundamental nature of God. No, this is all gift. God is free to give, and we are free to receive with thanks.

Worshipping God for his own sake, loving God for all he is worth, is a regular struggle of the scriptures. In fact, the whole of the book of Job could be seen as an investigation as to whether it is possible. You might remember it goes a bit like this: Job is a righteous man who is blessed in every area of his life: family, home, material possessions, influence and regard. He is, we are told one who, 'feared God and shunned evil' (Job 1:1). The opening scene sets up an ideal life for Job: 'he was the greatest man among all the people of the east' (1:3). You just know it's going to go wrong. The story cuts to heaven, and there we have a view of the Satan insisting that Job is only faithful to God because of what he gets out of it. 'Does Job fear God for nothing?' the Satan asks (Job 1:9).

The Satan is given permission to test him and see. So in a two-wave attack, Job is stripped of everything: the family die in tragic accidents, the livestock are wiped out, his buildings fall down and his body is afflicted with sores. By the middle of chapter 2 he is sitting among ashes scraping himself with a piece of broken pottery. Quite a downfall. Yet in all of it, despite his wife's protestations he refuses to curse God:

> Naked I came from my mother's womb, and naked I will depart.
>
> The Lord gave and the Lord has taken away; may the name of the Lord be praised.

> *(Job 1: 21)*

The rest of the book is about Job's love for God. Despite the pressure of his so-called friends, Job refuses to back down from his faith in God and his desire to hold out for him. The story ends with some of the most stunning poetry of scripture as God confronts Job in a way that doesn't answer any of his questions, but legitimises his faith.

I point you to Job, Gem, because I think at its heart there is something about worshipping God for God's own sake that goes against the grain or our culture. For we don't do anything except for selfish gain. The Sunday paper I read encouraged me into ethical living last month with ten reasons. The first was that I would feel better about myself. So I am not saying it comes easy or even naturally for us. But I think we do well to insist that God is God, and that praise of him is central. And we enter into it for his sake, on his terms, with no thought for ourselves.

The practical outworking of this week by week is that I think you should keep calling people before God's face to praise him. That when we gather together, you don't ask how everyone is feeling, whether people are 'up' for it or not. If you did, who knows what kind of answers you might get from those teenagers that gather week by week at St Laurence. No, instead it's a deliberate and intentional agenda-setting plunge into praise. We attend to God. However we feel. Whatever we bring. Whoever the week has been dominated by. This is God's time and it resets us. We are here for him. Not here for him for ourselves.

This instinct in us is one of the most natural things there is. Just as your daughter will search a crowd of people to catch your eye, just as you will immediately make for your husband when you walk into a room full of people in which he is present, the Spirit within us cries 'Abba' to God. But if the instinct is natural, the practice of it is learnt.

This is stuff we have agonised about as a community; how do we take responsibility for teaching young people to connect with God? How do we teach them these things without restricting them to simply doing it the way we do it? If we seek not to be relevant (a waste of time, resources, and the schoolboy error of letting the tail wag the dog) but to be authentic, what does it look like to enable these young people to worship God in a way that is authentic to them and to the orthodox Christian tradition in which they stand?

In terms of being authentic I think it means doing the things that Christians have always done when they have gathered together week after week: praising God, reading scripture, praying for others, confessing sins, sharing bread and wine. This is the content of what we do. You could say it's fixed. But the form it takes changes depending on the who, where, and what of each particular congregation and even each particular week.

So of course we use ancient words from the Psalms. Not primarily, as Eugene Peterson says, because they give us *carte blanche* to say to God anything we are feeling. But rather because they help us to answer God truly. We are tool-using creatures: cutlery and spades, keyboards and mobiles, cups and plates, toothbrushes and hairbrushes (well, some of us at least). And so with prayer, we use these ancient tools to enable us to know how to answer God, how to respond to him, how to address him truly.

Your task as the worship leader is to set these tools – which are gifts from God – out for the gathered community and then to show them how they might go about using them. And the best way of learning this is by being immersed in doing it. In her book *Glamorous Powers* Susan Howatch describes a priest explaining to his daughter what the point of set words in a liturgy is. He explains:

> It provides a structure which makes the task easier – just as your teacher made the task of learning to write easier years ago when she gave you specially lined paper to help you form your letters.

Now of course it isn't good enough just to wheel out stuff that has worked in the past. Sometimes the patterns and habits people get into with worship don't help them form letters; they simply give them a stencil which they are told they must never deviate from. But what if part of your task as the worship leader is to draw these lines so that young people can learn how to write and spell and express themselves to their creator and redeemer?

This then is the weight of the task. But what are some of the essential elements in seeing this realised? If wonder and praise, if worship and thanksgiving are shaped in the regular gathering of the community of the people of God, what might worship which is authentic to God look like?

Many times you've have been round to our house for a meal, and we've eaten well due to Belinda's kitchen swagger. She does sauces particularly well – you know the kind that start off very runny and bland, but after being reduced down over the space of a couple of hours become the basic essence of all the flavours. The basic essence of the flavour of the Christian faith is the simple but mystifying confession that God is Father, Son and Holy Spirit. And this makes all the difference in the world to how we worship.

At the heart of Christian praise and worship is the relationship of Jesus with the Father, which is enabled by the Spirit. (Even though that can sound clunky, it obeys a good rule of thumb – never refer to one member of the Trinity without an acknowledgement of the other two.) In our life in Christ we are caught up in this relationship – we are the children of God, we call God 'Father', Jesus is 'brother', we are the beloved of God, we are heirs, we are accepted, desired, held, resurrected. This is entirely a gift to us through the work of Jesus Christ.

In *Worship, Community and the Triune Grace*, which I think I once lent to you, Professor James Torrance accuses much of our worship of not being sufficiently Christian. He makes a distinction between Unitarian and Trinitarian worship. The trouble with many contemporary views on worship is that they are in effect Unitarian. Worship is something we do: we go to church to present our offerings, pray our prayers, and sing our praise. This is led by someone at the front. Rather, he says, worship is about gift: through the gift of the Spirit we are given the gift of participating in the incarnate Son's communion with the Father. Jesus is therefore the real agent of worship, and by the Spirit we participate in his offering to the Father, his constant prayers on our behalf. Trinitarian worship is not something we do; it is God who makes it happen. This means he is not only the object of our worship, but its enabler. God is the one who, through the Spirit, enables us to participate in Christ and all that he has done in the past, and all he continues to do for us now. In this scheme of things, the Spirit makes it all possible. Just as the smell of fresh bread that supermarkets pump through the air conditioning creates a desire in us for fresh bread, the Spirit brings to our senses the desire to praise God.

Now we are getting to the heart of things. Because this God is not an 'It', not a thing, not some inanimate force to bow before, but a life to be participated in. There is a dynamic here that tips us into the realm of the eternal. There is encounter.

My argument would be that worship of God has always been about encounter. From Jacob and his staircase to heaven (don't even start humming it), to Moses and the burning bush, to the dance of King David before the Ark, the Old and New Testaments are littered with descriptions of something which we struggle to describe adequately in words, because what is going on is a meeting with the Holy. We are told that in the New Testament this continues as the believers gather together and listen to the apostles' teaching, break bread and share wine, pray for one another and exercise the gifts God has given to them. What is going on when we worship is a meeting with the true and living God.

Now of course we want to hold that God is everywhere, the sustainer and upholder of all things. Those trees in the park opposite your house? The reason they stay up is because God upholds them. The breath your neighbours have as they protest there is no God, is a gift from God, a sign of his presence with them. So God is present everywhere. But there are times and places when there is a more concentrated sense of his presence. This is particularly true in worship.

The Psalms speak again and again of God's face: they implore God to turn his face towards us, David pleads that God turns his face from his sin, that the light of God's face turn to us. My favourite, Psalm 27, has a beautiful verse in it:

> To you, O my heart, he has said, 'Seek his face!'
> Your face, Lord, I will seek.
>
> (*Psalm 27:8*)

Face language speaks of presence. We can be in the same room as a crowd of people, present with them if you like, but when we are face to face with people we are 'present' in a different way. It is more concentrated, we are more present, if you like.

Praise is a dynamic form of conversation. So think about it like this; think of times when you have had conversations with people where they tore you off a strip, when they had a go at you, whether it was criticism or disapproval? When we have such conversations what happens to us? We are reduced, we contract, and we are almost shrunk by them. But think now of conversations you have had in which the person praised you – marriages are the best example of this. A person volunteers to name things about you that seek to verbalise your worth, to declare what you mean to them, and the things they value most about you. And they are not just saying it because they are trying to flatter you, being paid for it, or want something out of you. In such relationships we expand, and become more ourselves.

God is raised to his true excellence in worship only by the movement of God's own Spirit. Praise opens space for the recipient, offers to God space to be ever more and more true to himself, and serves to recognise the expansion which is God's nature. It is not that God expands to places where he had not previously reached, rather that, as Daniel Hardy says in *Jubilate: Theology and Praise*:

> God is in praise found to be ever more totally present;
> this is a profound intuition of the way he actually is.

In praise God is recognised and experienced ever more in the way he actually is. And worshippers find that his expanding nature becomes the means by which they 'expand' to become themselves, in this very relationship of praise. It is in this dynamic of the economy of praise that space is opened for God, for ourselves and others.

So my argument is that there is this human and divine meeting. It is not formulaic or mechanistic. God is free; there is no mechanical logic to it. But he is a God who loves to be present to his people. And day after day, week after week, he chooses to be present as his people gather before his face and praise him, listen to his word, confess their sins, bring their requests to him, celebrate his presence among them with sacraments, and share the gifts he has given them for the corporate body.

You probably know the story of the small girl who is sitting in the kitchen with her mum after school one day. She asks: 'Mummy, is God everywhere?'

'Yes darling.'

'Is he in this room?'

'Yes of course, he is with us now.'

'Is he right by me?'

'Yes, right by you.'

'Is he in this empty glass?'

'Um … yeeeesssss.'

The girl slams her hand over the empty glass on the table.

'Got him!'

And this has been the history of the church; attempting to control God, to reduce God's vibrant, living, life-for-us, to rituals, formulas, rules and practices. And that's true of Catholics, Protestants, emergent-types, Charismatics and Pentecostals.

God is free. Beyond any control or manipulation. But in worship the true God chooses to be what he longs to be for his people; present, for them. This means that the primary task of a worship leader is to seek to do justice to this God, an impossible task in some ways, but one which we are always able to be on the right side of. We seek to open up space for him in praise where he can be found and known to be ever more present. He is alive and interacting, true to himself and his ways, being all he says he is: loving, forgiving, speaking, urging, rebuking, encouraging, uniting, claiming, holding, releasing, giving, inspiring, quietening, healing, saving, reminding, declaring, freeing, binding, inviting, feeding, sending and blessing.

Writing of this is the only time in my life I have ever felt regret that I don't know more about jazz. Because it feels a bit like jazz – the spontaneity, the unknown, the vibe of life, the playfulness, the newness, the eternal variations on a theme, played by experts who know their instruments and their keys in every detail, and yet are free in the moment for whatever the music requires.

You will know that we have tried to build corporate worship not primarily for the individual, but around the community. The trouble is that our practice of music and our culture can mitigate against the whole community aspect. I don't know if you remember my friend Troy from Mars Hill, Grand Rapids, coming to speak at St Laurence. He had phenomenal insights (I keep urging him to write them down and get them published – when that book comes out it will be a must read). He set out before us that having personal music experiences was an unusually modern phenomenon. We are utterly used to fifty people sitting in a train carriage listening to their own individual music. This is made possible by all sorts of technology, from headphones, to iPods, to the ability to record music. But before such recording of music was possible everything would have been live, corporate, and on the whole, public. Music is most alive when it's live, and everyone is participating.

The participation of the community in worship is essential. That happens not simply through their presence, but through their activity. Namely singing. A song doesn't explain; it responds, it witnesses. It raises its voice beyond the timbre of speech, into melody and rhythm. Sung praise takes normal words, day-to-day expressions, and addresses them to God. And we do this together. On my own my voice is ropy and faltering, struggling to hold a tune – at least a recognisable one. Joined with others it lifts and grows, it shines and it contributes. They sing not only for themselves, but for me. I sing for the ones two rows back who cannot even bring themselves to raise a whisper, such is the week they have had. The person next to me is able to harmonise, bringing richness and depth to the sound. In all this we are not simply showing we are the body of Christ, we are being the body of Christ. In singing the corporate nature of the church isn't simply illustrated, it is realised. Our right place is alongside others, publicly declaring for all to hear who God is and what he has done for us. Our best prayer for anyone is that they come to praise and enjoy God more: 'Let everything that has breath praise the Lord.'

This is why the words that we sing are so important. There is a Latin phrase (I know, get me), '*Lex orandi, Lex credendi*' and the sense behind it is what you sing and what you pray is what you believe. We sing our faith. God's people always have done. The psalms tell of God's past actions and his present help, and look forward to what will one day be. And part of the power of them is they form in the worshipping congregation the framework for their faith.

In those monthly meeting we used to have we talked a lot about the kind of songs that we should sing at church. And I was always a bit grumpy about all the ones which seemed to have ourselves at the centre of them. I mean the ones that begin with 'I', which seem not really to be about God, but about ourselves and particularly our experience in worship. So we declare, somewhat aspirationally, 'I will give you all my worship', 'I'm coming back to the heart of worship', 'Here I am to worship', 'I lay my life down at your feet'. All great sentiments (although maybe it's a bit too easy to promise things which are a bit more difficult to deliver), but isn't it all a bit focussed on ourselves? In our self-obsessed culture, shouldn't Christian praise be mounting the charge away from the self, to God?

At its best this is what worship does. It unselfs me and sets me in a community before the face of God. Here we attempt to respond to all that God has done and is doing. Therefore there cannot really be any authentic off-the-peg worship, any more than what God is saying to one community through a passage will be the same as what he is saying to another. This is why video sermons baffle me – not simply because it is like watching fireworks on TV, or a DVD of a gig of a live band, but because what God is doing among one community in one place is different from what he is doing in the place down the road. No, worship is particular. It's about these people gathered in this place, going through what God has for them.

For this we obviously need a wider repertoire of songs; songs of lament that acknowledge hardship (over one third of the psalms fall into this category), songs that tell of God's work in history, songs that encourage us all to come before God, songs that prise open the future, songs that draw us to the most profound place of intimacy, songs that spur us to action, songs that reduce us to silence and leave us gasping for life. Of course the many question marks against 'Jesus is my boyfriend' songs are worth thinking about, although it's worth attempting to come to terms with the full-on love of the Song of Songs.

I always knew I should have encouraged you to write more songs. Worship is agenda-setting for the whole community, not for the spurious reason that it changes our moods, but because it embeds our beliefs and enables this gift of faith to 'take' in us.

So how should God's truth sound? What if praise is the soundtrack for our lives?

This is of vital importance because you become like what you worship. I give you Psalm 115:

Not to us, LORD, not to us
but to your name be the glory,
because of your love and faithfulness.

Why do the nations say,
'Where is their God?'
Our God is in heaven;
he does whatever pleases him.
But their idols are silver and gold,
made by human hands.
They have mouths, but cannot speak,
eyes, but cannot see.
They have ears, but cannot hear,
noses, but cannot smell.
They have hands, but cannot feel,
feet, but cannot walk,

nor can they utter a sound with their throats.
Those who make them will be like them,
and so will all who trust in them.

The clear insinuation in these verses is the trouble with worshipping idols is they dehumanise you. When things are worshipped instead of God, they steal our humanity. I haven't got enough time in this letter to set out anything more than the sketchiest of theories on idolatry, but it is the biblical contention that things God made good, when raised to a prominence they weren't made to have, do not expand us. but reduce us. Think of money, possessions, sexual desire, food, war, power, position. When someone worships an idol – and you can always tell if this is happening just by looking at the areas in which a person is making sacrifices – it diminishes them as a person. It affects their choices, their integrity, their freedom, their character. 'Those who make them will be like them.'

But the flip side of this is also the case. When we worship the God who made us in his own image, we become the people we were made to be. When we worship the true and living God, we become more truly alive, when we praise the generous and gracious God, we become more generous and gracious, when we adore the God who loves and gives, we become more loving and more giving. You become like what you worship.

Praise and worship are therefore places of transformation and change, times where we glisten with possibilities of what we might one day be, in fact what we will surely one day be. Just because it hasn't happened yet, doesn't mean that it isn't true. In worship this is imagined, anticipated, and celebrated.

But if these broad brushstrokes set out the arc above our heads, what are the potential threats to seeing this realised? I'm afraid they are numerous, too numerous to go into great detail, so I will earmark two: stoicism and the 'industry'.

Wonder gets squeezed out of us as we leave childhood. As a father, one of the most disheartening things to see in the girls as they grow up, particularly as they get towards their teenage years, is the fireblanket of cool that is thrown over any excitement. The giddy, delighted response to thrills which is such a natural joyful reaction gets underplayed because of the horror of looking overkeen before friends. We get used to things: we take sunrises and sunsets for granted, we hear of the birth of a baby without shedding a tear, we forget the wonder of the human body, we fail to remember that the light from some stars started travelling to us before Jesus was born, and we opt instead for coping, managing, and maintaining the equilibrium.

The stoics were those who in ancient times trained themselves not to show great emotion. No crescendos of joy, no crashing despair. There is much to be commended in this: it is patient and enduring, committed and brave, exhibiting self-control and a deep care for justice. But there is a lack of engaging with life as it is − weeping with the tragedy of it, and feasting with the celebration of it. There seems to be a fear of letting oneself go and truly experiencing life. This is a threat to praise. The form of Christianity it takes is full of rules and morality, full of hand-wringing about the state of the church, and full of fear for the future of the faith. It's full of head-down rationality which draws its boundary lines with clear stark marker pens. It feels colourless and rather inane.

Of course such stoicism is countered in some quarters by enforced joy. That won't do. That is equally unchristian. As David Ford writes in *Praising and Knowing God*:

> The agony of the joylessness of many communities and of the oppressive forms of 'joy' in many that pride themselves on their praise, is that it is starvation in the midst of abundance.

We are called, however, to be faithful witnesses to the God of joy and resurrection, the God of excess and overflow, of abundance and unending favour. This is the God who holds these over-whelming things out to us in the one hand, with a personal knowledge of suffering and godforsakenness, of betrayal and rejection, of pain and death in the other. If we are truly to witness to him, we do it best not by arguing with people, or haranguing them for their questionable morality, not by scaring them or manipulating them, but by declaring the praises of God who is from ever and for ever for them. To do anything else is to allow the world to set the terms and conditions for how the faith interacts with it. But God deals with us on his terms, so we can declare again and again; 'Let everything that has breath praise the Lord'. The biggest question isn't the problem of pain (although you and I know that one leaves us winded for months and years). No, the biggest question is why God chooses to love us as he does. And it's to this end that praise is directed.

The other threat to worship is, ironically, the worship industry. Now I will get my grumblings over quickly about inane tunes and insipid rhythms, about overproduction and dazed stadium anthems, about the lack of passion and the whole darn straight-down-the-middle-of-the-roadness of it all. We all have different tastes, I know and apparently, even though that means that some don't listen to Cash, Dylan, Springsteen, Elbow and the Mumfords, everyone's taste is valid. *Chacun à son goût.*

But apart from the plethora of continual new songs, the terrible poetry, the inane rhymes, the clichés, and self-centred lyrics, it's the 'industry' of it all. As that hero of mine, Eugene Peterson said in an interview with the *Church Times* in 2006: 'we have become consumers of packaged spiritualities. God is sold as a product. A cliché is as bad as a blasphemy.'

Now of course there many, many people who write songs and release records who are authentic and true in their worship. They have profound and inspiring love for God, which generates a reflective light in which we bask. I know some of the songs aren't to everyone's taste, and a few songs to Jesus seem to me like tasteless melted cheese. But it's all too easy to take a pop when actually the thing that offends us most is the depth of encounter and intimacy such songs express to Jesus Christ. When we have a go at the so-called Jesus is my boyfriend songs, I realise that I can sound like someone who is criticising a husband for serenading his wife with too-saccharine love songs. At least he loves her. Of course there needs to be balance and wisdom and poetry and reality and good theology and lament and passion and a few more chords. But it's the industry of it all that feels, well let's be polemic here, almost heretical. That album you bought, which when downloaded, had a message which you could transfer to your phone, which was a recording of the worship leader's voice as your outgoing voicemail message (grrrrr). The tweets encouraging us to buy the latest album so it can get in the iTunes charts, so we can make Jesus famous (grrrrr, grrrrr). The Facebook pages dedicated solely to the 'fans' of the worship leader (grrrrr, grrrrr, grrrrr).

So next time you are on one of those worship conferences, why don't you try sliding a list of questions such as these under the door of a couple of worship leaders:

- Do you have to have your picture on so many things?
- Why do you shoot a video of your songs? And when you do are you acting or worshipping?
- Could you stop doing album/DVD/book tie ins? Because isn't it just about making more money …
- Could you stop launching albums at big Christian festivals which up your sales (our teenagers keep falling for it)?
- Could we re-think worship tours? Is it right to charge people to come to praise God? What of those who can't afford the entrance fee? Are they not welcome to come and worship God?
- How do you decide what to do with the money you make from drawing people close to God?
- How about giving your music away for free?
- How about turning the big lights off on the stages, or at least the cameras?
- Next time they want to include one of your songs in the best worship album ever, could you say no and point them towards the psalms?
- You don't really think that just putting the word 'justice' in a song makes it holistic, do you?
- How about some songs of lament?

- If you met Jesus of Nazareth at one of the big festivals what do you think he would think of the worship?
- Could you listen to some of the aspirations of teenage Christians who want to be famous worship leaders?
- How do you think this culture has arisen?

To package and sell God, even if done with honest and good motives, destroys true worship. And therefore it destroys the church. Endless vigilance is needed, for as David Ford always used to say, the abuse of the best is the worst, or 'the best things invariably attract the most devastating corruption.' But too much is at stake here for us to sit idly by.

As for you, dear friend, keep leading young people and the whole of the community of St Laurence towards and before the face of the God who is worth loving and praising simply for who he is. Not for what we get out of it, but for his own sake. And as you encounter the true God you will realise yourselves to be truly transformed into who you were made to be.

I wish I could have seen what this will look like,

With grateful thanks,

Chris

9

Limelight

To Famous Christian Man

Famous Christian Man isn't real. Sure, you would recognise his image, associate him with certain events and initiatives, and maybe have bought a book because of his endorsement. But I am not talking about anyone in particular. And even though it's most likely that he is a he rather than a she, it's not always the case. So there can be no name on this letter. Rather, it's one that maybe could be left out in speakers' lounges at summer conferences.

But if it's not to any specific person, maybe it's not even to a group of people; maybe it's to the whole subculture of Christianity. The big stage, the names, the large projection screen, the bright lights, the Madonna-esque microphone, the glossy, glitzy, airbrushed culture of it all. Maybe this letter is to the whole machine which creates, produces and feeds Famous Christian Man.

It's about the healthiness of this limelight, not just for Famous Christian Man, not just for the subculture, but for the life of the Body of Christ – the impact that beguiling images, massaged egos and bright lights might have on our pure devotion and faithful witness to Jesus of Nazareth.

I'm writing this because I have been present when, during an interview on stage, in front of thousands, Famous Christian Man was asked what the church in the west needed, and he unhesitatingly answered, 'More people like me'. I'm writing because there is a gap between the projected image and the reality. I'm writing because this is dangerous. For everyone.

But to be honest, maybe the main target of this isn't Famous Christian Man, or the Christian subculture. Maybe it's to that part of me that still feels regret and failure that I am not Famous Christian Man myself.

Dear [insert name],

This story illustrates perfectly the desperate desire we have to make an impact without much thought of substance.

My daughters attend the same primary school. Trying to find out what goes on day by day is not easy. I have more idea of the workings of the Hadron Collider than the workings of the school. But the other Wednesday, over the spaghetti bolognese, the table talk flowed. Assembly had been one to remember. Some visitors had been in and had asked for two volunteers for a game. Typically Jessie, our six-year-old, had been chosen. Once in front of the whole school, she was given a very large pair of pants. The competition was to pull the pants up and down as many times as possible in 30 seconds. Jessie managed 29. Hooray. The boy (bigger, stronger, older) managed 31. Booo.

She didn't seem too disheartened, but as this point the parents round the table were trying not to look too concerned that their six-year-old daughter was in front of the rest of the school pulling a pair of pants up and down. The following conversation went something like this:

Belinda: 'Well, you obviously enjoyed that, Jessie.'

Jessie: 'Yes, mummy.'

Belinda: 'Did they say anything else … was there a point they tried to make?'

(Pause.)

Jessie: 'No, I don't think so.'

Belinda: 'Did these visitors say where they were from. Did they say, by any chance, they were from a church?'

Jessie: 'Can' t remember. But they looked like Yo Dudes. ('Yo Dudes' is an expression my daughters use to describe people who are on trend. When I asked them once if Daddy was a Yo Dude they looked at me with a mixture of amazement and deep sympathy.)

Hope (elder sister): 'Yes yes, they were from a church called …
called … called … Springsong.' (It honestly could be true.)

*Belinda (for at this point I've passed out and am lying on the floor
under the table with a faint moaning noise coming from my lips):* 'Are
you sure there wasn't a point to the pants games?'

Hope (remembers and declares rather triumphantly): 'Yes, yes there
was. Everyone has got a gift.'

Belinda: 'Right. And how do you think the game helped show
that?'

Hope: 'That Jessie has got a gift of pulling her pants up and
down?'

Now I have done assemblies in my time that have involved
eating flowers, cat food and shaving foam. I have dressed up,
made toast, pretended to be deaf and staged clapping competi-
tions. And, while I have never actually used pants, I have done
things which have fairly loose associations with any points I want
to make. But my daughters' assembly begs so many question I
will have to save most of them for our family therapy session in
ten years' time. Suffice it to say for now: how has it all become
about style over substance? Why will we do anything to try and
be memorable? Why do we seem so desperate to be relevant?

If one thing is true of the western culture of which we are
part, it is surely that consumerism isn't just the blood pumping
through our veins, it's the very heartbeat of everybody. The
analysis and implications of this in wider society, the cost and toll
it takes on us, the effects and demands it makes on us, have been
explored and highlighted by those far more insightful than I. (I've
been particularly challenged by *The Beauty Myth* by Naomi Wolf,
No Logo by Naomi Klein, *Empire of Illusion* by Chris Hedges,
Affluenza by Oliver James and *The Secret of Happiness* by Alain de
Botton.)

My particular concern is how these market forces so obviously
and unquestioningly dominate the mainstream Christian culture.
In *Working the Angles* Eugene Peterson rails again and again at the
preoccupation Christians have:

> We are preoccupied with shopkeepers' concerns – how
> to keep the customers happy, how to lure customers

away from the competitors down the street, how to
package the goods so the customers will lay out more
money.

However, from the start I want to recognise the true calling of
God on the lives of men and women to be leaders. I want to
affirm that God clearly gives women and men strong and astonishing gifts with which to serve him and his people. And that
many men and women sacrifice a huge amount in the godly
exercising of their ministry. I have friends who haven't married
because they have singly pursued the calling God has given them
in the exercise of their gifts, those who have paid a price
financially and relationally, and those whose health has suffered as
they pour themselves out for others. It is not that to lead isn't a
valid or necessary vocation. It is that this vocation needs to be
exercised with the greatest candour and care; not only does the
leader have a responsibility in this, but so do all those who are part
of the Body of Christ. If one of the most profound and godly
communicators on all things spiritual of the last century, Henri
Nouwen, sensed that his 'success' was putting his soul in danger,
he might not be alone in the feeling he wrote about in *In the
Name of Jesus*;

> Too often I looked at being relevant, popular and
> powerful as ingredients of an effective ministry. The
> truth is that they are not vocations, but temptations.

In this letter I will set out where those greatest temptations press
hardest on a Christian leader and cause damage which can act like
a virus on the Body of Christ. Taking the temptations of Jesus as
the framework, we will look at each one in turn; the temptation
to be relevant, the temptation to perform, the temptation for
power through untruth. As well as exploring each of these, I will
suggest an antidote which is stronger than the virus. Our model
will be to be an image of the icon and follow the footsteps of Jesus
of Nazareth. To be those whose corporate life is harmonious with
how he lived, what he stood for and what he stood against. My

fear, as I look at myself and the Christian culture I am part of, is that too often we mirror the society we are part of rather than the saviour who saves us. This can cause us to look like bent police officers, like firefighters turned arsonists – betraying the very thing we say we stand for by our actions and words.

The story of Jesus' temptations is as profound a narrative as we get in scripture. It's one of those passages which might only take eleven verses to tell, but the scope is cosmic. A story which, if it had it gone differently, would have changed everything. Unique among the stories of Jesus' life, it is the only one for which there were no eyewitnesses for any of the details, causing us to realise, with a sharp intake of breath, that we only have this account because Jesus himself related it to his followers. Such was its importance.

It takes place directly after the baptism of Jesus, as he is driven, or in the Greek sense of the word, catapulted, into the desert.

> After fasting forty days and forty nights, he was hungry. The tempter came to him and said, 'If you are the Son of God, tell these stones to become bread.'
>
> Jesus answered, 'It is written: "People do not live on bread alone, but on every word that comes from the mouth of God." '
>
> (*Matthew 4:2–4*)

The first temptation, to turn stones to bread, is no heinous crime. Jesus hasn't eaten for weeks; he is malnourished and painfully weak. There is clearly nothing wrong with the suggestion of eating. Indeed, in his future ministry Jesus will feed hungry people. But at the root of this and every temptation is the questioning of Jesus' identity: '*If* you are the Son of God', something that has just been affirmed at his baptism, immediately prior to this event. The heart of this temptation is the lure that he should not go through hardship, but prove himself and use his gifts to meet the obvious need. That is; he should prove himself relevant.

How often have we wished we could do this – to meet and fulfil the presenting need with miraculous provision? To show how relevant being a child of God was for the things that most obviously faced us? Could any of the rest of us reject this temptation?

Our Christian subculture is littered with claims and gimmicks pleading relevance, with attempts to show how presenting needs are met and fulfilled. And I wonder if the desire to be relevant, to say the important things, to meet the essential needs, partly comes from our desire to justify ourselves.

In his wonderful book on the spirituality of the desert mothers and fathers, *Silence and Honey Cakes*, Archbishop Rowan Williams quotes the harshly named John the Dwarf: 'we have put aside the easy burden, which is self-accusation, and weighed ourselves down with the heavy one, self-justification.' For there is no end to carrying self-justification: 'there will always be some new situation where we need to establish our position, dig the trench for the ego to defend.' The craving to justify ourselves is insatiable.

Christian leaders feel this acutely, so one of the things we do with it is baptise it. We make it about God. We do it in God's name. Is it just me or is the strap line 'Living to make Jesus famous' more than a tad distasteful? Is this really what Jesus needs us, wants us, calls us to do? One church has taken this to the nth degree and adopted the strap line, 'Jesus needs better PR', which might be hilarious, if it didn't turn our stomachs. The ever-astute Craig Borlase lashed out in a blog post (read his books too):

> Do we think God's the foreign exchange student in the corner, all acne and awkwardness, just desperately waiting for someone cool enough to come along and validate him with our approval? Would it all be better if only God got a little better at making himself attractive? Does God have an image problem? If so, you can bet it's all our fault.

I fear the aim of 'living to make Jesus famous' shows us at our worst. For one thing, it reveals we haven't let the one we serve dictate how we serve him. Why do we think he cares about being famous? He is the one who laid everything aside, taking the form of a servant, making himself nothing (Philippians 2:7). He didn't care a jot for fame when he walked the earth, in fact he walked in the opposite direction away from the limelight. For another, we betray some of our true motives; might it not be us we want to make famous, and is Jesus is our vehicle for doing it?

So Jesus gets co-opted to our need for self-justification. We report what we are doing and what God is doing as exactly the same thing, stitching ourselves into his picture time after time. We become so self-referential that we make ourselves essential. It's *our* products that are really going to help people, it's at *our* conference that people will really encounter God, it's at *our* church where his healing will truly be experienced, in *our* teaching that his voice will most clearly be heard. Again Rowan Williams warns in *Silence and Honey Cakes* that:

> … one of the greatest temptations of religious living is the urge to intrude between God and other people. We love to think that we know more of God than others; we find it comfortable and comforting to try and control the access of others to God.

But again behind it all, isn't there this monster of self-justification prowling round to devour us? We, like those who came to Jesus time and time again, want to justify ourselves (Luke 10:29). I have spent time in school rooms chatting to insecure teenagers and in seminar rooms observing the sense of inferiority among post-graduate students, but the sense of fear at being inferior and not quite flavour of the month has never been more palpable than in the speakers' lounges at Christian conferences.

As a culture we seem to have an obsession with how we will be remembered, with leaving a legacy. One of the fears we have about death is being forgotten, so we want to make a splash. So when the thief dying on the cross next to Jesus asks to be remembered, we comprehend his desire: 'Please, dear Jesus, remember us, ensure that our lives will have a significance, so we will be remembered.'

However there is something, no, in fact everything, about the death of Jesus that frees us from having to make something of ourselves, for we are not thrown back on ourselves: our own resources, our own justification, our own efforts. Actually I don't think the thief is trying to grasp at some significance. He has simply recognised that Jesus is truly the only one who can remember, or as Stanley Hauerwas says in *Cross-Shattered Christ*: 'like the thief, we can live with the hope and confidence that the only remembering that matters is to be remembered by Jesus.'

What if Jesus could take from us our need for self-justification, either by gently prising our fingers open or smuggling them open and stealing from us that which ruins us? This can happen particularly when we come before him alone, when we come not with our achievements or the things others say of us, but as ourselves. Everything is stripped away.

The antidote to our craving for relevance is being face to face with God; that is prayer. In prayer I am offered the gift of coming clean, for here the curtain is ripped down, the masks are laid aside and I am truly known. Here I am addressed by the word that I cannot truly live without. Here, I attune my ear to listen to the words that proceed from the mouth of God. Here, in confession, I die to myself, I lay down the burden of having to make something of myself. For we exist, 'because something has happened which makes the entire process of self-justification irrelevant' (Williams again). On our knees our egos are minis-tered to; for here we are loved, not for what we give but who we are, not for what we bring but simply because we come. Here we are not massaged or given false praise, but confronted with the real Jesus who takes from us all of our pretentions: to be the messiah, to be the answer, to be the relevant ones. Here we are reached, accepted without qualification, undone and in our undoing, made whole.

Early on in my ministry I experienced falling under the weight of expectations from others. It deeply saddened me that I found myself letting people down time and time again. I laboured under it, so went to talk to Michael, a wise elder friend. He listened gently and then observed that I could learn a thing or two from John the Baptist. When people go to him and ask if he is the messiah, his response is that he is not. Michael said to me: 'Chris, the good news is you are not the messiah. Jesus is. The trouble is, you will meet and serve those who want you to be. And worse still, you will find yourself wanting to be the messiah to others. But always be clear, you are not.'

In prayer I am asked questions by the God who fixes me with his loving, knowing, unflinching gaze. In *In the Name of Jesus* Nouwen talks of these questions being not those we ask ourselves: how many people take us seriously? How are the results going? How effective do we think we are? But the question that Jesus asks Peter three times in their post-resurrection encounter on the beach is 'Do you love me?' The weight and poignancy of God's questions remake us and redeem us. Here we can be ourselves, which is who we are and are called to be. Nouwen again:

> I am convinced that the Christian leader of the future is called to be completely irrelevant and to stand in the world with nothing to offer but his or her own vulnerable self.

—ɯ—

> Then the devil took him to the holy city and had him stand on the highest point of the temple. 'If you are the Son of God,' he said, 'throw yourself down. For it is written:
>
> He will command his angels concerning you,
> and they will lift you up in their hands,
> so that you will not strike your foot against a stone.
>
> Jesus answered him, 'It is also written: "Do not put the Lord your God to the test." '

(*Matthew 4:5–7*)

The second temptation for Jesus is to go to a religious place and perform a miracle. Once again this enticement to go to godly places and there produce something out of the ordinary, in the name of God, is far too close to the bone. But clearly this temptation is to do something that works, something that impresses, something that turns heads and makes an impact. As with the first temptation, at first glance there is nothing heinous about this temptation. I mean, no one is losing their life, are they?

But actually, they are. For here, the audience's entertainment is the motivation; to do something impressive is the goal. Here, amongst the cheering warmth of approval, you win the world, but forfeit your very soul. Performance is a killer. And not just for those who perform, but for the whole of the church's identity and mission.

Of course there are good reasons for wanting to perform well; note how the Satan is able to quote scripture to back up why Jesus should perform the impressive miracle. But Jesus knows that if he starts by giving into the pressure of doing impressive things to gain a following, he will find all the excuses in the world not to go through the agony and suffering of dying on a cross. I mean, who wants to follow that kind of messiah and saviour? The Satan knows that if Jesus falls for this one, the taste of playing to the approval of the crowd will be sown and enticing him away from the cross will be easy.

For the trouble is, in terms of performance, it trusts that the tastes of the crowd are right and true and give an accurate measure of what we should be doing. History is littered with terrible examples of the wants of the people being served by the most horrendous actions and regimes. We are fickle, fickle creatures.

Now two things need to be said; firstly that things done in God's name should be done well. God deserves our best. Secondly, that by necessity in the cultures we inhabit, we engage with all sorts of ways with all sorts of media. Just consider the things amplification and new opportunities for travel make possible. And we haven't even mentioned the interweb or the like. I have given up on the self-promotion of Twitter and the Facebook posts telling us you are just going into Number 10.

But, to my knowledge at least, very little thought is given to the effect using the media has on us. In his seminal book *Flickering Pixels* (anyone and everyone in leadership or seeking to communicate in Christian faith should read it) Shane Hipps, who before ordination in the Mennonite church was a senior advertising executive for Porsche, sets out to slay the mythical dragon that we have an unchanging message which we simply need to use modern media to communicate. No, he argues, following Marshall McLuhan, the medium you use to communicate the message doesn't simply affect the message, it becomes the message itself. He illustrates this wonderfully by charting the impact the printing press made on what we believed the gospel was and how it was understood, and even how church buildings were designed. It is particularly his perspective on image I'm thinking about here.

For images affect us in an entirely different way from words. A different side of our brain interacts with them, they capture our imagination and bring definition in a unique way; they make us feel, not think. They don't invite us to argue or debate, they give us an experience. A picture is worth a thousand words. Furthermore, our relationship to those whose images we recognise is bizarre; we think we know them because we recognise them, they are familiar to us.

Because images are so powerful, they are highly controlled by those who produce them. In our culture celebrity is daily trading in illusory images. The belief that the camera never lies was only possible in a generation before Photoshop. The impact of video and moving images on our culture has inadvertently been to create celebrity. 'We used to have heroes; now, thanks to moving images, we have celebrities' (Shane Hipps again.) This is not to say that we should throw away projection screens, DVDs or anything with an image on it; I'm merely making a plea to the subculture that serious thought is given to use of images and what is being portrayed. If we are in any doubt, the power of an image is reflected in the second commandment; that we should not make false images.

Whether on a screen or in a published photograph, images offer us a person as a product. And it's the place for this product which I wonder about at times. Of course products are not simply visual; we deal in words and ideas, in disciplines and desires. What I wonder is if there is, maybe just sometimes, an integrity gap sometimes between the product, the thing being offered, and reality.

It is in the immense wisdom of the Church of England that before they ordain a man or woman they send them away on retreat in the days immediately preceding the ordination service. So in late June 1996, I found myself with thirty-two others, some of us due to be ordained deacon, some, now twelve months on, to be ordained priest. These were days of silence and contemplation, of rousing 'eve of battle' speeches by the bishop, of sincere prayers and desperate 'staring into the whites of your eyes' moments when I wondered what on earth on earth I was doing. On the Saturday night, with all the intensity over, we were encouraged to relax. Most of us sloped off to the local pub, where we all sat sharing our fears and asking those who had been at it for a year already for their advice. They had completed a year of ordained ministry and were back for more. Out of everything that was said on my ordination retreat, it is only that conversation in the pub I remember.

It all started when one of our number shared how hard she found it to pray on her own. What she was worried about wasn't so much leading a congregation publicly in prayer, but her own life on her knees in private. The floodgates opened, as those ready to be Priested the next day chirped in: 'Oh, don't worry about that, I was ordained last year and haven't prayed on my own since then.' 'I can top that,' boasted another, 'I haven't prayed on my own for five years. But I can lead people in church. It's just a role, isn't it? Just leading the performance.' I left my drink and fled back to the retreat house. Part of me wanted to beat the bishop's door down and insist he talked to these pretenders, so livid was I that these people were just performing some role. But the intensity of my reaction was dread and fear, because I knew I could easily become like that. How easy it is to project an image of myself as one thing, but in reality to be something very different.

Being one thing before others and another thing on our own is a temptation many of us face. It is terrifyingly easy to say something once because you meant it, then to keep using it because it went down so well the first time. To pray prayers in one context for a particular person, which seemed to hit the right note, and so to keep using them because, well, they sound so impressive. To use tones of voice, gestures, stories, phrases simply because they add to the performance.

Personally I am convinced that God speaks in many and varied ways all the time to us for each other. I delight in being part of a church tradition that expects God to say specific things to specific people at specific times. These are usually known as words of knowledge, pictures or prophetic insights. But I also know what my friend Abigail means when she says that too often they are 'words of general knowledge'. For sometimes, just sometimes, in such times of waiting for specific things God might say, often called 'ministry times', I see, at best, a desire for people to respond, causing those leading them to fall back on patterns and ideas that have 'worked' before, and at worse, manipulation, affected learnt behaviours and what I would have to call religious abuse. The third commandment outlawing taking God's name in vain isn't about swearing; it's about using God's name to endorse your own point of view, your own standing, your own performance. And that makes me shudder.

I think about prayers I have prayed publicly that I have not believed, easy answers I have given to complex questions which didn't do justice to people, and certainty communicated when what was needed was an invitation to the mystery of faith. About motions gone through, inspiring anecdotes regaled, and moving stories reused. And all, really, so I would come out of it looking good.

My blood runs cold when I consider Bob Hope's maxim: 'Sincerity is what matters. Once you can fake that, you've got it made.'

Rather than simply repackaging past products, wheeling out things that worked well in the last meeting or pushing buttons that are a dead cert to bring results, isn't the fact that God is the living God, constantly doing new things, engaging with us in fresh ways, first hand, our greatest challenge? Isn't it the case that learnt techniques too easily seem to sell God and his things as a product, and keep us from the true encounter that changes our lives? Eugene Peterson writes in *Working the Angles:*

> I don't want to live as a parasite on the first-hand spiritual life of others, but to be personally involved with all my sense, tasting and seeing that the Lord is good.

This attention to the aliveness of God is what we need. Consider two stories in Luke's Acts of the Apostles.

In Acts 12 Peter is locked in prison for his witness to Jesus Christ. He is being guarded by soldiers; everyone is praying. An angel comes to him and he is freed, leading to the comedy moment where he arrives at the door of the house where they are praying for his release and the girl who answers the door is so surprised to see him, she shuts the door in his face. 'Wonderful', we cry, 'God releases the captives', 'look at the power of prayer …'.

Four chapters later Paul and Silas are in prison; as they are singing and worshipping, there is an earthquake. The prison doors open and their chains drop off. 'Wonderful', we cry, 'God releases the captives', 'look at the power of worship' and they leave the prison having been freed by God. Oh, hold on, it's a different ending. Paul and Silas stay in the prison, even though they could leave. 'But Paul, imagine the testimony you could get on the back of that one, I mean it could pay your air-ticket around the world, what a story.' But Paul and Silas somehow know that what is happening with them is different from what happened with Peter. One is freed to leave, the others are freed to stay. And because they stay, the jailer and his family come to faith and probably form the backbone of the church in Philippi.

My point is that in each situation they do not second-guess God. They do not assume they know what he is doing. They recognise he is doing different things; freeing Peter from prison in one but asking Paul and Silas to remain in prison in the other. Throughout scripture there seems to be no thought about performance. Simply an alertness and aliveness to what God is doing.

—⁓—

Again, the devil took him to a very high mountain and showed him all the kingdoms of the world and their splendour. 'All this I will give you,' he said, 'if you will bow down and worship me.'

Jesus said to him, 'Away from me, Satan! For it is written: "Worship the Lord your God, and serve him only." '

Then the devil left him, and angels came and attended him.

(Matthew 4:8–11)

The third temptation is to bow down before the Satan. It says it has been given the kingdoms of the world. It lies. And it promises power based on lies. A shoddy deal done out of sight that offers Jesus power without any suffering. On this Henri Nouwen writes in *In the Name of Jesus*: 'The temptation to consider power an apt instrument for the proclamation of the Gospel is the greatest of all.' And there is of course much that could be said, and probably needs to be said, about our relationship to power.

However what I wonder about is this unreal world that the Satan exists in: a world where he is in charge rather than the real world where God is due all glory. It's a place where truth is compromised for the sake of power.

And so I wonder, Famous Christian Man, about truth, about those blurred edges between what is a real story and what is a made up one. I wonder about hype. about numbers that are rounded up, then up again (in our house we joke about 'evange-lastic' figures), about the most optimistic hope being dressed up as a promise of what God will do, and about 'names' endorsing books they haven't even read.

In the past few years there have been particularly difficult revelations about those whose story had been triumphantly told from stages. There have been those who have flown round the world because of their powerful stories of healing, miraculous provision for their need, or their struggle with debilitating illness, which have turned out to be fabricated. Such miracles, hardships and amazing stories have turned out to have been rooted in a desperation for approval and the applause of the crowd. Particular instances do not concern us, but what is concerning is the part that the whole subculture has played in creating the conditions for such falsehood. In his book *Under the Unpredictable Plant: An Exploration in Vocational Holiness* Eugene Peterson has coined the term 'Eccelesiastical Pornography' to describe much of the sub-culture's self promotion and air-brushed claims.

In *Silence and Honey Cakes* Rowan Williams asks:

> What if we could recognise people of faith by how they spoke? By an absence of cliché or of dehumanising mockery or glib consolations ... the times when we can be absolutely sure we are wasting words are when we are reinforcing our reputation, or defending our positions at someone else's expense.

And as Van Morrison sang in 'Wonderful Remark': 'How can we listen to you when we know your talk is cheap?'

This then is a call to consider how a microphone is used, how a stage is placed, how words are written. It's about the lips and feet and hands that do this. And that it's not about a product, but about a person. And who we are isn't about what we produce, but our character.

This call to me to give attention to my character needs to be heeded on every level. Not simply because what we build with our gift we destroy with our character. Not simply because who we truly are is what we communicate; if I am talking to you about measles, but I actually have chicken pox, what you will catch from me is chicken pox. People catch who we are. That's why we don't believe those who tell us God loves us just the way we are when they are dressed from head to toe in designer labels.

Giving attention to our character is a primary vocation for everybody who embarks on the journey of following Jesus. The formation of character is painstaking and is a long-term discipline. It is a life's work. My sense is Jesus spends the first thirty years of his life preparing himself in the secret place for what he is called to. He is only able to resist temptation because of the decisions and disciplines he has previously made and honed. His prayer, his rigour in attending to his father, his delight in creation, his love for others don't just drop into him. These are cultivated in his character.

It is in my personal choices, disciplines and habits that my character is shaped. For example, I know that my promise to my wife to be faithful is kept not simply in the moments that I find myself in the eye of the storm, confronted with a woman who I could be unfaithful with, but in the choices I make with my eyes, desires, imagination and will day by day.

The following story about a surgeon in the 1960s is from *The Shape of Living* by David Ford. It makes me gaze into the sky for minutes upon end – you'll need to pour yourself a coffee for this one …

> I was visiting my friend, Dr Guy Badenoch one
> afternoon at his home in George Square, Edinburgh,
> and I mentioned to him how sad I was over the death
> of a child in the operating theatre of the nearby
> hospital. I went on to say that I felt great sympathy for
> the doctor who had been in charge of the operation
> since he had encountered an unexpected complication
> and could hardly be blamed for what had eventually
> happened. To my astonishment Dr Badenoch, a just and
> understanding man, replied:

'Oh, I don't know about that, Donald. I think the man is to blame. If anybody had handed me ether instead of chloroform I would have known from the weight it was the wrong thing. You see, I know the man well. We were students together at Aberdeen, and he could have become one of the finest surgeons in Europe if he had given his mind to it. But he didn't. He was more interested in golf. So he just used to do enough work to pass his examinations and no more. And that's how he has lived his life – just enough to get through, but no more, so he has never picked up those seemingly peripheral bits of knowledge that can one day be crucial. The other day in that theatre a bit of 'peripheral' knowledge was crucial and he didn't have it. But it wasn't the other day that he failed – it was thirty years ago, when he only gave himself half-heartedly to medicine.

It goes without saying that I found Dr Badenoch's words a hard comment, and I do not know if in this particular case they were justified. But fundamentally he was right: for almost a lifetime we may project an image of ourselves that enables us to get through, that deceives others and may even deceive ourselves. In the end, however, what we are always comes out; it is for what we are that we are responsible.

We cannot, then, accept a definition of character that it is merely 'who we are in the dark'. No it is who we are in the light, it is how we treat the stranger, the unwelcome, unwanted guest, the homeless person crossing our path, the friend who has let us down, the angry child, the stroppy teenager, the airline attendant who loses our luggage, the shop assistant who tests our patience with their go-slow attitude.

My trouble with the limelight is that the spotlight, as Shane Hipps writes in *Flickering Pixels*, 'magnifies talent, but not character'. It leads teenagers to have the ambition to be recognised and prominent, rather than to be godly. It encourages lone rangers, not being part of the body of Christ.

Such formation of character happens only in community. This is where we live out the incarnation; the call is not simply to live in my physical body, but with this corporate body of people, in a community where I am known, where I share my life, where my weaknesses and failings are painfully obvious, where I can get shouted down if I start exaggerating to come out of a story better, where I can be held to account for the grand pronouncements and schemes I launch. Here the rhetoric finds its balance, the soaring comes down to earth. Here the captured, airbrushed image is refocused onto a group of people who live not for themselves but for others.

In his *Letters and Papers from Prison*, the modern-day saint Dietrich Bonhoeffer writes of meeting a man who confessed his ambition to be a saint. Bonheoffer was initially mightily impressed with such a desire, but on reflection felt there was something that didn't sit right. He wrote a few months before his execution; 'One must completely abandon an attempt to make something of oneself, whether it be saint, or a converted sinner, or a churchman, or a righteous man'. Rather, we should live as part of the people of God in the world, being a corporate group for others, together providing a way for the coming generation to live, caring for those who are left washed up by the culture, a voice for the voiceless and a place of belonging for those who are excluded. It's this rootedness in community that is salvific in our culture for those who exercise up-front ministry. In *In the Name of Jesus* Henri Nouwen shares his experience in the North American church:

> One thing is clear to me: the temptation of power is greatest when intimacy is a threat. Much Christian leadership is exercised by people who do not know how to develop healthy, intimate relationships and have opted for power and control instead. Many Christian empire builders have been people unable to give and receive love.

A story is told of a man who hated his work in a factory, but as it was a time of great unemployment he had no choice but to stay at his job. Every lunch hour he would go down into the cellar, take his hammer and chisel and hew out a brick from the foundations of the factory building. He would put it in his bag and walk out of the factory gates, disposing of it on his way home. After five years of him doing this, one night the factory mysteriously collapsed. If you don't have a brick in your bag to undermine the building, you are keeping it up.

Famous Christian Man, and all involved in this Christian subculture, it might be that none of this is true for you. If so, that is wonderful. These could simply be temptations I, as a church leader, know the heat of. However it might be that you recognise parts of the caricature in yourself and others. But it also might be that you feels the game has gone on so long that there is too much at stake to do anything particularly radical about it all. My plea is that we all take responsibility for ourselves and for the environment we create to communicate and nurture faith in, that it and we would be appropriate to Jesus of Nazareth. That we would be faithful witnesses.

So keep putting bricks in your bag and be careful about the glare of those lights,

Chris

10

Imagine

To Sammy

Sammy is a chirpy chappy, especially when given chocolate. He is the third child of friends of ours at St Laurence.

On 11 October 2009 I baptised Sammy when he was just two years old by full immersion in the fifteenth-century font at the entrance of the church. Apart from the fact that I hadn't quite thought through water displacement, it was a very moving occasion as generations of his family, and the whole of the church gathered to celebrate this ceremony of him becoming a full member of the church.

I love baptising the children of God at any age. But for me there is something particularly special in baptising a child; it speaks of the accessibility of the grace of God, of the value that children have in the life of the church, and in the investment in the future that the church of today is called to choose for.

So this letter is to Sammy. It's one written as if on the day of his baptism, which carries an ache, a dream and a hope of what he might be part of when he brings his own children to baptism.

Dear Sammy,

I am writing this to you on your baptism day. You'll be pleased to know, for the record, that you didn't cry, you didn't have to wear a dress and the whole of the front row were soaked, including your grandmother. Please do apologise to her (again) from me. As I am sure your parents will show you the photos and the cards, this letter isn't about telling you what happened; this letter is a foretelling of what I hope might be.

That might sound a bit weird, like an attempt at fortune telling. But that's not my intention in writing it down. My strong conviction is that baptism states things, claims things and enacts things in categorical ways. So I guess all I am trying to do in this letter is imagine what those stated, claimed and enacted things mean for you, who you will be, and what you will stand for.

Today, 11 October 2009, is your baptism day. Some will think you got unnecessarily wet, but it is a day of great rejoicing. And not because the bouncy castle your parents hired kept us all amused for hours, or because your mum sang karaoke after the dessert, but because of what had just taken place, and the difference that made to your future, and the future of others. For what went on today wasn't just some bygone rite of passage, the traditional thing to do if you still happen to be connected to church – this is the stuff of life.

In your baptism we are doing something in the now, the present. We are stating loudly and deliberately that you are a vital member of the church of Jesus Christ. Not that one day you could be a member when you are old enough to read a lesson at the front of church, or when you are able to take some responsibility, but now. This day. We stated that you are as important as any adult in the community of faith.

But true Christianity is never one-dimensional; it's never simply about the now. It looks back and roots everything on the strong anchor of God's work in history, particular in Jesus Christ. And it anticipates a future, God's future. It doesn't simply hope for it, in the way you hope for a winning horse to come in, or that your dad might finish that kitchen extension in the next decade. It makes it possible. It brings it into being.

Baptism is an ancient practice. It can be traced back to the New Testament, and to John, who was so prolific a baptiser that he got a name from it. Jesus is baptised by John and John is then imprisoned. No more is said of this ceremony until after Jesus has returned to heaven and God sends his Spirit to his people, when those who get caught up in the new life want themselves to be part of it. How do they get in on it? How do they become members of the people of God? They are baptised. Right there in the middle of Jerusalem. And ever since then every church (bar the Quakers) has baptised those who want to count themselves in. In the last 2,000 or so years the practice around baptism has changed in fascinating, and sometimes eye-brow-raising, ways. But what hasn't changed in that a person's baptism is held out as the time they sign up officially for being part of the community of Jesus Christ. Even if they are too young to hold the pen themselves.

Baptism finds its roots in the historical event of Jesus' baptism. It's a short story, so worth writing out in full:

> When all the people were being baptized, Jesus was
> baptized too. And as he was praying, heaven was opened
> and the Holy Spirit descended on him in bodily form
> like a dove. And a voice came from heaven: 'You are my
> Son, whom I love; with you I am well pleased.'
>
> (*Luke 3:21–22*)

In the river Jordan, which marked the boundary to the land the Jewish people believed God had given to them as their own, their 'promised land', Jesus went into the water along with everyone else. They were entering the river because they wanted to show the new start they wanted to make. They wanted to be washed, to be cleaned, to be free from their life of rebellion against God, so they could be free to embrace God in their future. It identified them as those who wanted to live God's way.

Today you were baptised into Jesus Christ. You become a participant in him, because in this baptism event of his, he became a participant in your life. He participated for you, he lived for you, suffered for you, died for you, rose again for you. Your identity is his. His identity is yours. This is the kind of stuff I mean when I say, baptism states, claims and enacts. Because today we stated, claimed and enacted that you never stand alone. That you stand in him.

It is not that you bring anything to this is make it a possibility, or to make it happen. You simply come to the waters. There has been many an argument about the kind of person you need to be in order to be baptised, the optimal age you have to be to be baptised, the background you need to be from. In fact it started happening within a generation of the church being born. And it was quite a row. It seems St Paul was quite partial to a bit of a row.

You should be very grateful that Paul won the argument in the early church. The book of Galatians, from which we read on this your baptism day, addresses a church which is in complete crisis. Paul had started a church in the area of Galatia (part of Turkey these days – ask your parents to take you there on holiday). The people were non-Jewish (Gentiles, as they are known), but they had come to believe and had been baptised, presumably by Paul himself. But after his exit from Galatia he was followed by representatives from the church in Jerusalem (the Jewish-leaning church) who argued that if the new converts really wanted to live their lives as Christians they had to be circumcised, to follow the Jewish law and observe the Jewish religious traditions. Paul heard about this and went nuts. Baptism doesn't baptise a person into a life of religion, into rules and rituals, into i-dotting and t-crossing observance; it is baptism into freedom.

Paul won the day with his insistence that becoming a Christian didn't mean becoming a Jew. If he hadn't, today would have been much more painful for you, although you would always look back and have some gratitude towards your parents that they had you baptised as a child rather than waiting.

But seriously, it would have been far more than just painful on this level, because this would have ghetto-ised Christianity. The only people who would have been able to be counted as the people of God were people who had undergone this, who were male, and who were Jewish.

Baptism is, as Paul says, altogether different. For here is a rite, a practice, a celebration which everyone can take part in. So as Paul says in Galatians 3:28: 'there is neither Jew nor gentile, neither slave nor free, neither male more female, for you are all one in Christ.'

This is one of the reasons that it's brilliant that you are the age you are today – it speaks of this inclusiveness of God. You're in. There are no height charts for gaining entry into the kingdom. You can never be too young to be part of the family of God. We prayed these words together. They are ancient ones, loaded with meaning:

> Samuel, for you Jesus Christ came into the world:
> For you he lived and showed God's love;
> For you he suffered the darkness of Calvary
> And cried at the last: 'It is finished.'
> For you he triumphed over death and rose in newness of life;
> For you he ascended to reign at God's right hand,
> And there he prays for you now.
> All this he did for you though you did not know it yet,
> and so the word of Scripture is fulfilled,
> 'we love because God first loved us'.

For you, Samuel, are on equal ground with the young orphan girl who was baptised today in Rwanda, with the illiterate grandmother who was baptised today in Argentina, with the teenage Afghan refugee who has found a true home while fleeing, with the child of royal birth in St Peter's Basilica. This is something Judaism with its circumcision could never do. But the ground around the cross of Jesus is level.

Sadly, you will realise fairly quickly that throughout the history of the church people have loved measuring others with tables of merit and ladders of significance. I am sorry to say that this verse will be as radical to the church when you are my age as it is now: that women stand on equal ground with men, that those who are poor are on the same level as the rich, that gay men and women stand in the same full force of the love of God as straight people. And while, shamefully, it may be the case that the church of Jesus Christ is still attempting to realise this verse when you are my age, I charge you to be a champion of this wonderful, level playing field.

You can do this because of your identity as one 'in Christ'. This is the term used in the New Testament, far more than the one we use so often, 'Christian'. Your identity then is set, by your baptism. But the water won't stop a myriad of identity thieves trying to poach it. As it's true today, Sammy, I am guessing it will continue to be true, and probably to gather in pace; your identity will be fairly relentlessly under attack.

Some of the attacks on our identity come under the guise of significance. We are obsessed with being significant. And this is nowhere seen more clearly than in our desire for celebrity. Alarmingly, I heard the other day that when a group of twelve and thirteen-year-olds were asked what they wanted to be when they were older, 70 per cent of them replied, 'famous'. We are obsessed with fame. Our lives gain significance from the brushes we have had with celebrity (you will have heard the story about your mother bumping into Diana Ross). 'We are waiting for our cue to walk onstage and be admired and envied, to become known and celebrated.' (This is a quote from a book I lent your parents by Chris Hedges, called *Empire of Illusion: The End of Literacy and the Triumph of Spectacle*.) This desire for celebrity ruins our identity as we attempt to acquire significance.

Others construct an identity by taking on a persona or a character. You can buy one off the peg. You can reinvent yourself time and time again. Of course not without cost, or without losing yourself in the chaos of it all. So take, for example, the internet. My guess is it's here to stay. And even though I would like to see its demise, Facebook seems to go from strength to strength. On Facebook we all create our own identities. We present who we want to be, who we want people to perceive us as. I tell you about the books I am reading so you can be impressed that I am the kind of person that reads *War and Peace*. I tell you about the films I've watched so that your opinion of me is enhanced, because I watch those subtitled ones. I share the latest lesson I was able to teach my children, all the time under the illusion that what I am doing is showing people who I really am.

But I am simply looking into a screen that has become a mirror, and not a true mirror which shows me myself, but one on which I construct a false image of myself. I am presenting myself to you as I want you to see me. Which is fine as far as it goes, as long as I and you don't believe it.

This means that my identity is constructed in public. I tell you everything; there is no private and public. I tell everyone what I felt like this morning when I woke up. Hey can I just share that my child is the cutest in the world? Goodness, my wife has just been diagnosed with cancer. It is a sign of the sickness of our corporate identity that we don't know any longer how to be private. We want to let it all out, because if we have 'felt' it we are justified. Why else would a mother of a five-month-old tell us that she had had such a hard night with a sleepless baby she was 'thinking of giving her baby up for adoption'. In what world would you share that fleeting thought with over five hundred friends? A world in identity breakdown.

But your identity is not in need of being constructed, simply grown into. Baptism gives you clothes which are always a couple of sizes too big to grow into, an identity to realise, a reality that constantly needs to 'take' in you and for you. And that identity is one of being beloved, one who is 'in Christ'.

Baptism enacts this, not simply in a way that illustrates words, and not simply in a way that declares with a symbol what we would otherwise use words for. To do that to this sacrament is to misunderstand the nature of the gospel. The gospel isn't an alternative way of thinking, or a new set of ideas, an alternative way of looking at reality. The gospel is a declaration that because of this man everything has changed. And those who are 'in Christ' are the ones in whom this change is realised. Baptism declares that you are one with Jesus of Nazareth, and so you too can hear the voice of the Father through his ears: 'You are my son, whom I love; with you I am well pleased.'

You are loved, Sammy. Loved as the Father loves the Son. Loved from before all time to the end of all time. So much of the time we spend a ludicrous amount of effort and time on constructing identities so that we might be loveable. But the trouble is, as the identities we construct aren't the true us, of course we never feel truly loved. But in Jesus you are loved as you are. You are loved strongly and relentlessly, faithfully and without any reservation. Your God does not watch you undecided, he does not wait to be convinced, the jury is not out. The verdict in Christ is unflinching and irreversible. He is for you. Always. Without hesitation, deviation, but with endless repetition.

You are loved. Loved not because of what you have done, or will do. Loved not because of being right or being true. Loved not because of what you have achieved or will achieve. But loved because you are the creation of the creator, the son of the Father, the one on whom his favour rests. While these things are easy to say, you will find, Sammy, that they take a lifetime to grasp. Or are we grasped by them?

Prayer helps us get there. From your earliest times you will grow up calling God 'Father'. The Spirit will form in you these words and this intimate relationship that each of us holds as our most dear possession; intimacy with a God who is intimate with us as he was with Jesus. We ache to hear these words again and again. And like your namesake Samuel in the time of Eli (1 Samuel 3), as you learn to hear God's clear words, make your prayer as his, 'Speak Lord, for your servant is listening ...' For these words will proclaim your identity as a beloved son each day.

A wonderful American preacher called Brennan Manning says that when we stand before God in judgement his question to us will be, 'Did you believe that I truly loved you?' For all of us, the question is, as I heard a professor of Divinity at Cambridge ask in the middle of a talk to students; 'What does being loved this much by Jesus do to your heart?' What does it do to our lives, to our security, to our attitudes, to our identities? It sets them free.

Now everyone longs for freedom. It is doubtful whether this desire will have abated or been fulfilled even when you die. We long for it. Why? Because it's this we were made for – it's in our genetic longing. It's part of the image we bear.

Today you were baptised into Jesus Christ, in the name of the Father, the Son and the Holy Spirit. This God is free. Free to be and free to love. Not made to do anything, not subject to outside forces or manipulation. His free choice for us is that we too should be free. So he forms us in his image, to be free. His strivings for us are for our freedom, he longs that we be liberated and all his activity in our lives is to lead us to that place.

We, however, have the somewhat fatal assumption that the price we pay for God's freedom is our slavery. We cannot conceive how he can be free, and we can be free. This is because we are under a desperate misunderstanding of what it is to be free. We assume it is the 'freedom' to choose to do anything we want.

Rather than have some philosophy-lite discussion on freedom, let's consider the freest man who has ever lived, Jesus Christ. Here is one who certainly didn't enjoy many of the freedoms we assume are an essential part of a free life. He was not free politically; he never voted or exercised his country's right for self-governance; in fact he lived in an occupied country. He was not free economically; he did not have the money available to him to enable him to live to a standard we would assume was the fruit of freedom. He was not free to travel; in his whole life he went barely seventy miles from his home town. His movements were restricted by the occupying force and by his economic capability. In short, he grew up in an oppressed country, poor and restricted. What's more, it is clear that he felt compelled in his sense of vocation to embark on one course of action. He chose to be bound and imprisoned, captured and tortured. He gave himself to face the death of a captive. But he did this freely.

'No one takes my life from me … I lay it down.' He freely chose to bind himself to fulfil his vocation. And in death he showed himself to be most free, as he was free to choose, not for himself, but for others.

Here then are some different strains of the freedom song. What if freedom isn't about the ability to be able to choose to do anything you want to do? What if freedom is being free to love? What if the thing that most imprisons us isn't our lack of funds, our lack of democratic rights, our access to information, or our ability to move around, but our inability to truly love?

Jesus came to us, having few of the freedoms that we, rightly, so highly prize, and lived a stunningly free life. And the root of his freedom was in his identity as the Son of God. He knew that he was the one who was loved by his father. He was entirely sure of it. And because he was so secure in the love that his Father had for him, he was free to love people. He was free because he didn't care what others said of him, he was free from having to construct, prove or defend his identity. He talked with prostitutes, aware that the establishment was looking on with horror and insinuating that he was probably sexually involved with them. He shared the table with the traitors to the nation who were tax-collectors, aware that in the eyes of the establishment he was now heavily compromised. He was free to associate with everyone, because he was not trying to get people to like him. He knew he was loved, and so people could say what they wanted. He will went about freely fulfilling his vocation, even when it cost him his life.

The thing is, Sammy, as much as we want freedom, if we choose to find it our own way we always come a cropper. The defining story in the Old Testament is the story of liberation from slavery in Egypt to the promised land. The people of Israel were slaves who were put to work to make bricks without straw. They could do nothing to free themselves. By the time you are six you will probably be really familiar with this story – no doubt you will have been dressed as Moses and put in a basket, coloured in the burning bush, pretended to have walked through the Red Sea and cut out cardboard and painted it grey to look like the tablets of stone the commandments were written on.

The people of God, his 'sons', as God calls them in Exodus 4, are called out of Egypt for freedom. Moses leads them out as the plagues have changed Pharaoh's mind eventually, particularly the most horrendous of all – the death of the firstborn. The children of God are spared this because they have smeared the blood of the lamb on the crossbeams of their doorposts; they run for it and pass through the water of the Red Sea. Then their journey through the wilderness to the promised land begins. En route, forty days later at Mount Sinai they receive the law. Think mountain, clouds, fire, smoke. But what was made for the journey of liberation became slavery.

Paul introduces the idea that the law – rules of behaviours and practices – was simply meant as a 'pedagogue' – the teacher of a young child in that same book of Galatians. The law was meant to look after these children in their infancy until the messiah arrived. It was to prepare and keep the people of God ready for Jesus, like a babysitter. Instead it became a thing of enslavement; Paul says that people are locked up in it, trapped in it, held in prison by it. You can never obey your way to freedom.

Samuel, watch how people will want to drag you back by being your babysitters, into having to do stuff to get God's attention or love, or truly be counted in. I remember vividly a conversation I had with a sixteen-year-old at church a week before she was due to be baptised. She had become a follower of Jesus from a really difficult background. Home was hard, school was harder, and relationships with men were devastating. She had been sexually active since the age of twelve, usually with men double her age. In the middle of our conversation about her forthcoming baptism she reached out and grabbed my arm: 'Are you telling me that if I get baptised next week I can never sleep with anyone until I am married?'

What could I say? I didn't want to peddle cheap grace to her; the life she was going to embark on as a baptised member of the community of faith would be marked by costly choices. But what conditions should I attach to her baptism, and those of others who were bracing themselves for the water? Should I ask to see Nick's bank balance and insist he subsequently send me all future statements? Should I put up a camera in Lucy's home to make sure she wasn't gossiping? Should I insist that Eloise start to be kinder to herself?

The demand on our baptised lives is that we live out our identities as those who are in Christ. That what he says goes. This is a process which takes all of our lives. But our means of entering it? Merely that we are slaves who long to be freed.

Life apart from this Jesus is slavery. Slavery to yourself, your own unfulfilled hopes and fears, slavery to codes of how to be and what to be, slavery to the power of idols and those who would be gatekeepers of freedom. Jew and Gentile alike are slaves. But God's drive to bring freedom is stronger than any chains of slavery. And his drive to bring freedom isn't a paper exercise; it's not notional, involving a new way of thinking. It's actual, because he achieves it.

I sketched out a little of the ancient freedom story of the Exodus; now we need to superimpose Jesus onto it. Because freedom comes not by Moses but by this Jesus; Galatians 4:4 states: 'when the time had fully come, God sent his Son, born of a woman, born under the law.' This law, as we have seen, brought slavery, yet Jesus comes under and into it. And he does so to redeem us from it. He becomes what we are so we might become what he is.

Think back to the story of Jesus being baptised. He is not alone; there are many with him. But they are all being baptised as a sign of their desire to turn from the things they have done wrong. It's called repentance. Jesus has done nothing wrong to turn from, but there he is in the water, being counted amongst the wrongdoers. If you were watching this scene from the back, you would assume that Jesus is just another man wanting to change his ways.

This free choice of his to be counted as one of us sets him on the route to his cross. I say his cross, but it would be more accurate to say it's our cross. This is the one person who didn't become death. His submersion in this river that marked the entrance to the land of promise and freedom, that God's 'sons' passed through hundreds of years earlier at the end of their great Exodus. Here the true Son passes through the water in freedom, but by doing so he enslaves himself to the consequences of all slavery; death. He freely chooses this because he loves us. But what is going on here is a liberation movement on a far greater scale than the Exodus. Because it involves the liberation of every person who has ever lived.

Freedom came for God's people in the Exodus, as the plagues devastated Egyptian society, particularly the final most bloody one, the death of the firstborn. The price of slavery is again extracted as the blood of the innocent lamb of God streams down the wooden crossbeam, as the plague of the death of the firstborn son takes place once again. But this time God takes it on himself. Freedom doesn't come for free.

But the people can now go free. Running for dear life, they pass through the water of baptism and journey to freedom. This freedom takes some getting used to; it is not always easier or as comfortable. There are temptations to return to Egypt. But why return to slavery when you have been freed? Of course this freedom is not fully known, not realised, not grasped immediately, just as the first Exodus journey to freedom took forty years, but free we are and we journey each day towards the promised land.

Here is freedom. Freedom from having to make something of yourself, freedom from having to construct your identity, freedom from having to liberate yourself, freedom to belong to God's people simply because you are loved, freedom from the things that hold and bind and enslave. It is this freedom that you have passed into through the waters of baptism. It is now your birthright. Enter into it. Grow into it. Practise it and live as if it is the truest thing about you. Prize it highly. Don't give it away.

Stand for this freedom, Samuel – don't let yourself be compromised in the beautiful ease of the gospel which says you are loved and all you have to do in return is mumble 'thank you'. The thirteenth-century mystic Meister Eckhart said: 'If the only prayer you said in your whole life was "thank you," that would suffice'.

What it looks like for you to live freely is an unknown to me. If I started to prescribe what freedom would look like for you when you are, say, a teenager, I would probably just be repeating some dreary stories from my adolescence. No, you must be free to embrace God's future for you, confident in the fact that he will constantly and consistently choose to be for you. But for me to give you advice on this, is like Saul giving his cumbersome armour to the young David when he was about to fight Goliath. It would be totally unsuitable.

But Sammy, as the future is cast before you, however you wear your freedom, wear it for the sake of others. Your identity as a freed one, is to be for others. We are freed *for* things. So be one who lives freely and generously in insisting that the loving kindness of God has acted to free everyone. And this is not based on their background or their social standing, their morality or even their response. Everyone has potentially been freed. Our task is to bear witness to what has taken place, and alert an enslaved world. We find our significance in doing significant things for others.

Freely embrace your vocation to live your contribution. There is something that God did in making you and freeing you that is unique and unrepeatable. There are things only you can do, gifts only you can bring, perspectives only you can share, goodness only you can spread. But do this in the context of a community. The people of God, those who bear his name, are those who have entered into this freedom to be for others. It is amongst these people, in the reality of our lives and the push and pull of our days, that the conditions for freedom are created. We as your church community will do our best to model it, to seek to live it and see it become true for you, as we do for everyone. But for that you will need to take your place, every year of your life. By your baptism today, we have marked your public joining of the community of faith. It publicly declares you to be part of the family of God.

This day is a celebration of the freedom of the children of God. You are a liberated child on this freedom train. You are on board. Your mum, dad, brother and sister travel with you; help them and us to see where we are really going. Encourage people not to get off the train and try and make their own way to freedom; help us to see where we are headed and be glad about it and, if you see people who want to get on, hold out a hand to them and urge them to come on board.

So today I find myself looking up at the corner of the room that I stare into when I don't know what something will look like, but am desperately desiring to see it. Imagine what you will be with this as your heritage, Sammy. Imagine the kind of church you can be part of shaping that lives this as its truth, and imagine the instrument of liberation to the world that such a community can be. But imagine it with joy, not because it is a dream, but because it will one day be.

It is not too much to want this,

to insist on this
to expect this,
to see this,
to taste this and to witness to this.

Ask your mum or dad to explain any of the bits you don't understand. I reckon they get it better than me.

Live freely,

Chris

DARTON · LONGMAN + TODD

We believe it is impossible to understand
the world if you do not understand what
drives the human heart and the human
spirit. DLT books will not tell you what to
think. But they might change the way you
see the world, and they might even change
the way you live.

Our books are written by, and for, people
of all faiths and none. We believe that
spirituality and faith are important to all
people, of all backgrounds, and that the
wisdom of any one culture or tradition can
inform and nourish another.

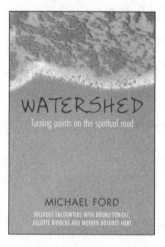

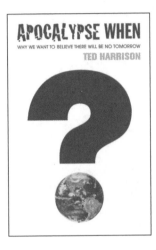